CONTENTS

M000239697

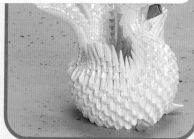

The Basic Triangles

Fat rectangle (such as 1½" x 2¾", 2" x 3½" or 1½" x 2¾" piece)

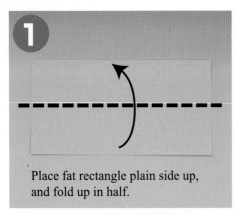

1 Place fat rectangle plain side up, and fold up in half.

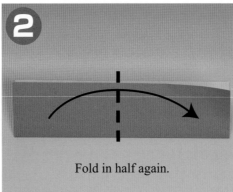

2 Fold in half again.

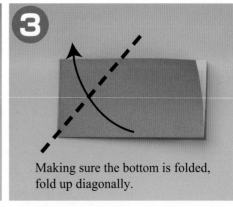

3 Making sure the bottom is folded, fold up diagonally.

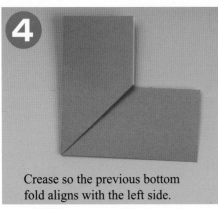

4 Crease so the previous bottom fold aligns with the left side.

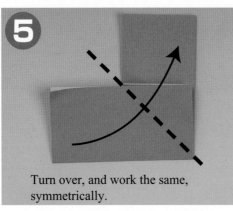

5 Turn over, and work the same, symmetrically.

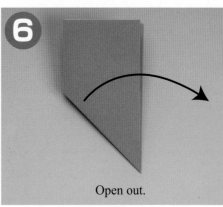

6 Open out.

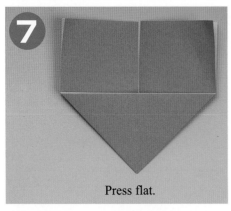

7 Press flat.

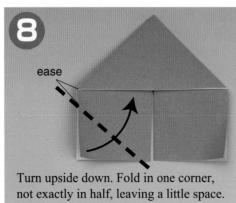

8 ease

Turn upside down. Fold in one corner, not exactly in half, leaving a little space.

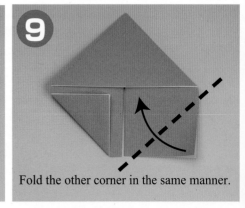

9 Fold the other corner in the same manner.

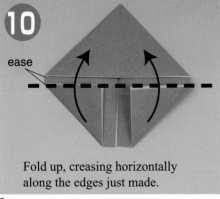

10 ease

Fold up, creasing horizontally along the edges just made.

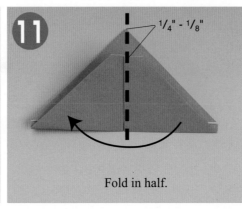

11 ¼" - ⅛"

Fold in half.

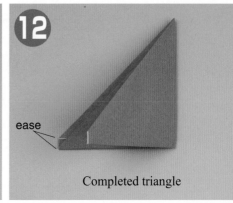

12 ease

Completed triangle

We have come up with three different ways to fold the basic triangles. The triangle is made from a rectangular piece, and the ratio of its short side to long side creates a subtle difference of overall texture of the project. Find out which size of paper you have in hand before dividing it into rectangles. For cutting each type of rectangle, see page 5.

Thin rectangle
(such as 1" x 2¼", 1¼" x 3" or 2" x 4¼" piece)

1

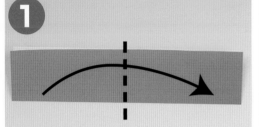

Place thin rectangle plain side up, and work in the same manner as opposite page until Step 7 is done.

2

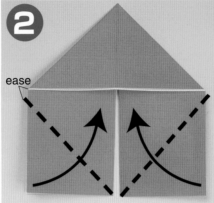

Turn upside down. Fold up corners, not exactly in half, leaving a little space above, and making pointed bottoms.

3

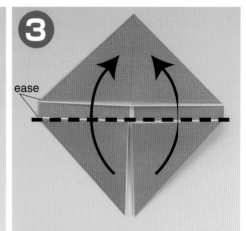

Fold up, creasing horizontally along the edges just made.

4

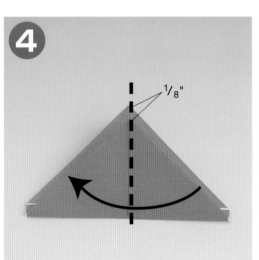

¹/₈"

Fold in half.

5

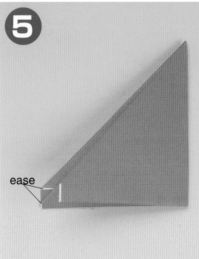

ease

Completed triangle

Half-square rectangle
(such as 1" x 2", 1⅛" x 2¼ or 1½" x 3" piece)

1

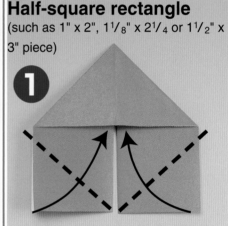

Work in the same manner as opposite page until Step 7 is done. Fold up corners diagonally, leaving a little space at sides.

2

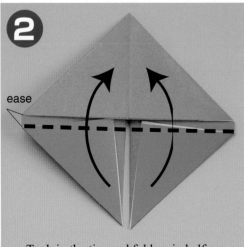

ease

Tuck in the tips and fold up in half.

3

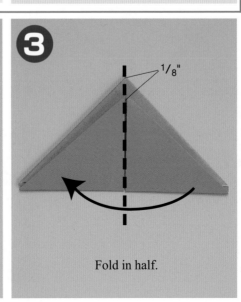

¹/₈"

Fold in half.

4

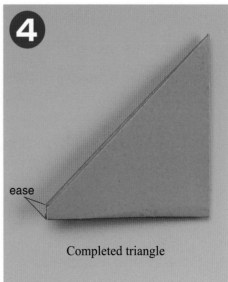

ease

Completed triangle

3

The Triangle Structure and How It Works

Anatomy of Magic Triangle

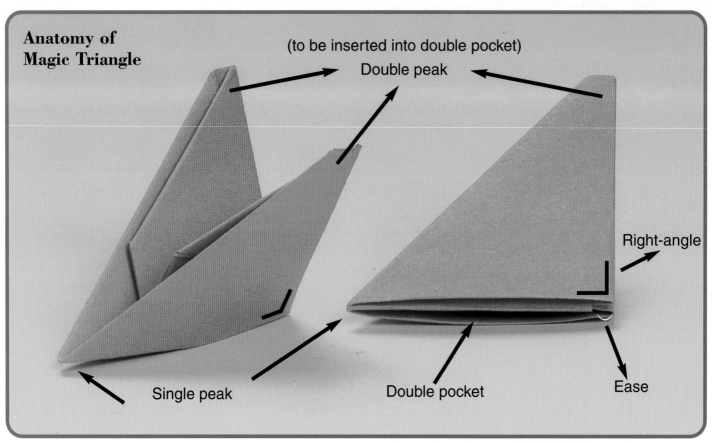

(to be inserted into double pocket)

Double peak

Right-angle

Single peak

Double pocket

Ease

Assembly

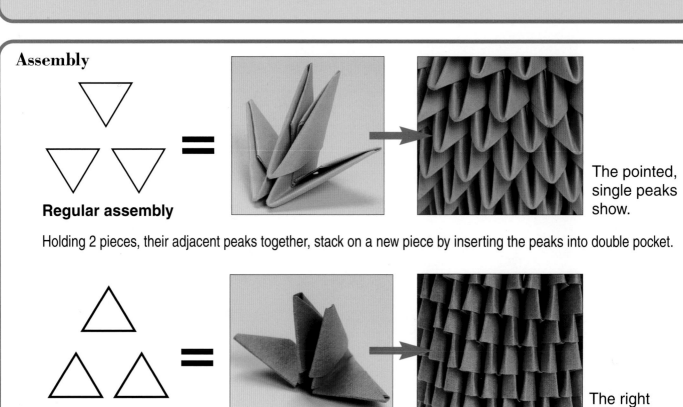

Regular assembly

The pointed, single peaks show.

Holding 2 pieces, their adjacent peaks together, stack on a new piece by inserting the peaks into double pocket.

Reverse assembly

The right angles show.

How to Cut Paper Efficiently

Commercial rectangular papers cut for 3D origami are available at craft shops. However, you can recycle used catalogs, wrapping papers, magazines and flyers to make the rectangles.

Cutting into rectangles

Cut any B-size or similar ratio paper into rectangles as shown, and voila! You can make 24 rectangles at once. Prepare and save ample numbers of rectangles before starting actual 3D construction. Divide into "fat" rectangles and "narrow" rectangles in order to create smooth surfaces.

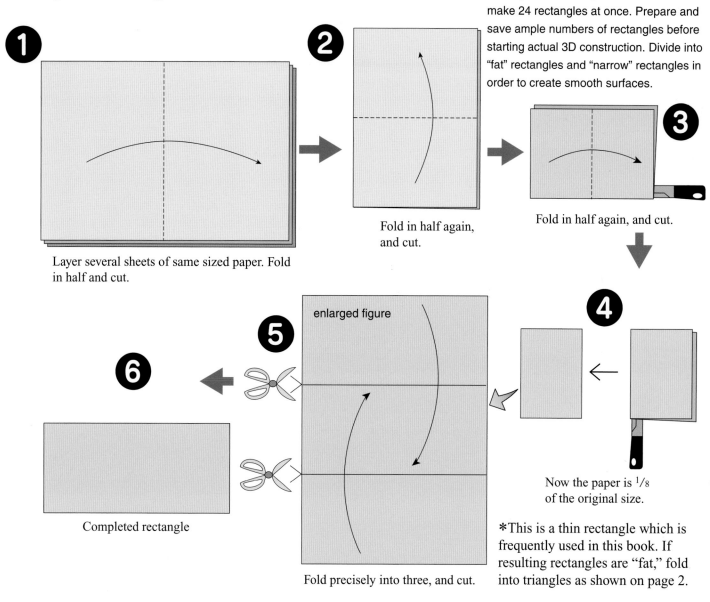

1 Layer several sheets of same sized paper. Fold in half and cut.

2 Fold in half again, and cut.

3 Fold in half again, and cut.

4 Now the paper is $1/8$ of the original size.

5 enlarged figure — Fold precisely into three, and cut.

6 Completed rectangle

*This is a thin rectangle which is frequently used in this book. If resulting rectangles are "fat," fold into triangles as shown on page 2.

Using Origami

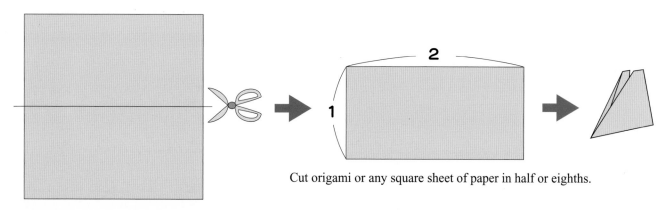

Cut origami or any square sheet of paper in half or eighths.

Beginner's guide

Chubby Chicken

Learn how the triangular pieces are assembled together as you create a 3D chicken. A gradated paper is used here to give a soft feather-like impression.

Head

1" x 2"

1¹/₂" x 2³/₄"

Make a cone with yellow paper, and cap as beak.

Materials per Chicken
366 1¹/₂" x 2³/₄" rectangles*(gradated shade)
3 1¹/₂" x 2³/₄" rectangles*(red)
2 1" x 2" rectangles*(red)
1 ³/₈" x 2" rectangles*(yellow)
2 ¹/₄" plastic joggle eyes
Fold rectangles* into triangles.

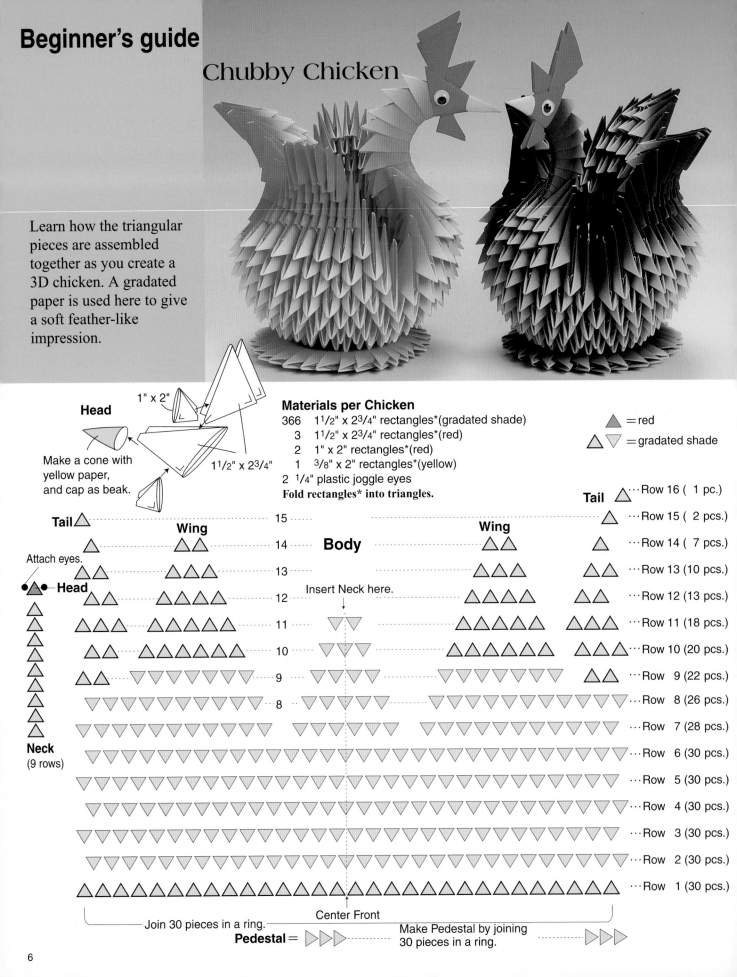

△ = red
△ ▽ = gradated shade

Tail △ ··· Row 16 (1 pc.)

Tail △   △ ··· Row 15 (2 pcs.)

Wing   **Body**   **Wing**

△ △   △ △   △ ··· Row 14 (7 pcs.)

Attach eyes.

△ △   △ △ △   △ △ △   △ △ ··· Row 13 (10 pcs.)

●△●—**Head**   Insert Neck here.

△ △   △ △ △ △   △ △ △ △   △ △ ··· Row 12 (13 pcs.)

△   △ △ △ △ △   ▽ ▽   △ △ △ △ △ △   △ △ △ ··· Row 11 (18 pcs.)

△   △ △   △ △ △ △ △ △   ▽ ▽ ▽   △ △ △ △ △ △ △   △ △ △ ··· Row 10 (20 pcs.)

△   △ △   ▽ ▽ ▽ ▽ ▽ ▽   ▽ ▽ ▽ ▽   ▽ ▽ ▽ ▽ ▽ ▽ ▽   △ △ ··· Row 9 (22 pcs.)

△   ▽ ▽ ▽ ▽ ▽ ▽ ▽ ▽ ▽ ▽   ▽ ▽ ▽ ▽ ▽ ▽ ▽ ▽ ▽ ▽ ··· Row 8 (26 pcs.)

△   ▽ ▽ ▽ ▽ ▽ ▽ ▽ ▽ ▽ ▽ ▽ ▽ ▽   ▽ ▽ ▽ ▽ ▽ ▽ ▽ ▽ ▽ ▽ ▽ ▽ ▽ ··· Row 7 (28 pcs.)

△   ▽ ··· Row 6 (30 pcs.)

Neck
(9 rows)

▽ ··· Row 5 (30 pcs.)

▽ ··· Row 4 (30 pcs.)

▽ ··· Row 3 (30 pcs.)

▽ ··· Row 2 (30 pcs.)

△ ··· Row 1 (30 pcs.)

Center Front

Join 30 pieces in a ring.

Pedestal = ▷ ▷ ▷   Make Pedestal by joining 30 pieces in a ring.   ▷ ▷ ▷

6

Chubby Chicken Assembly

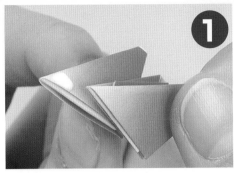

1 Make bottom row. Simply layer 2 pieces and stick with a dab of glue applied onto one peak.

2 Repeat with another piece, until 5 pieces are joined. Secure with a clothespin and let dry. Make 6 units.

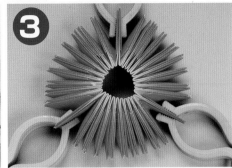

3 When the glue is dry, join them in the round, and secure with glue applied only to the peaks. Avoid separating glued pieces when using clothespins.

4 Work Row 2. Insert 2 adjacent peaks of Row 1 into double pocket of a new piece, the single peak facing out this time.

5 Repeat until all the peaks are covered and interlocked. The single peaks form a larger outline than Row 1.

6 Work Row 3 to Row 6 in the same manner, always interlocking adjacent pieces of the previous row with a new piece.

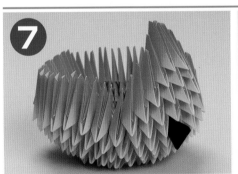

7 Form breast. Pick center piece, and join 3 pieces each on left and right, 6 pieces in all. Continue until Rows 7 to 11 are formed, decreasing 1 piece on each row.

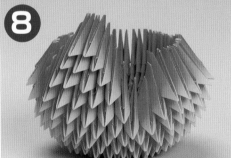

8 Make wings. Leaving 1 piece unworked on each side of the breast, join new pieces for Row 7. Work Row 8, decreasing pieces.

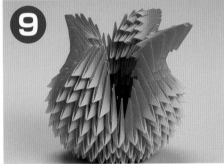

9 Make wings and tail, referring to the diagram on opposite page. For the tail, be sure to increase pieces on Rows 10 and 11, and then taper off.

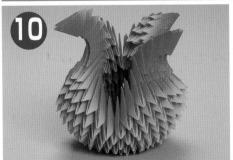

10 Make neck. Join 9 pieces flatways. Add to the breast, and bend into a curve to face forward.

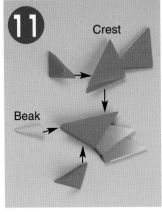

11 Crest

Beak

12 Pedestal (page 6)

11 Remove 2 top pieces off the neck. Join 1 red piece to the top to make head. Referring to opposite page, make crest and beak, and insert into the head.

12 Put the head back to the neck. Attach eyes. Make pedestal and place the chicken on it.

Good Luck Objects

Stacking each little triangle one by one for to build a good luck ornament is like making a wish for the recipient of your gift. 3D origami projects are heavyweight and stable, not like ordinary origami projects that are destined to be thrown away. Save wrapping papers or calendars and reuse them to create a heart-warming gift.

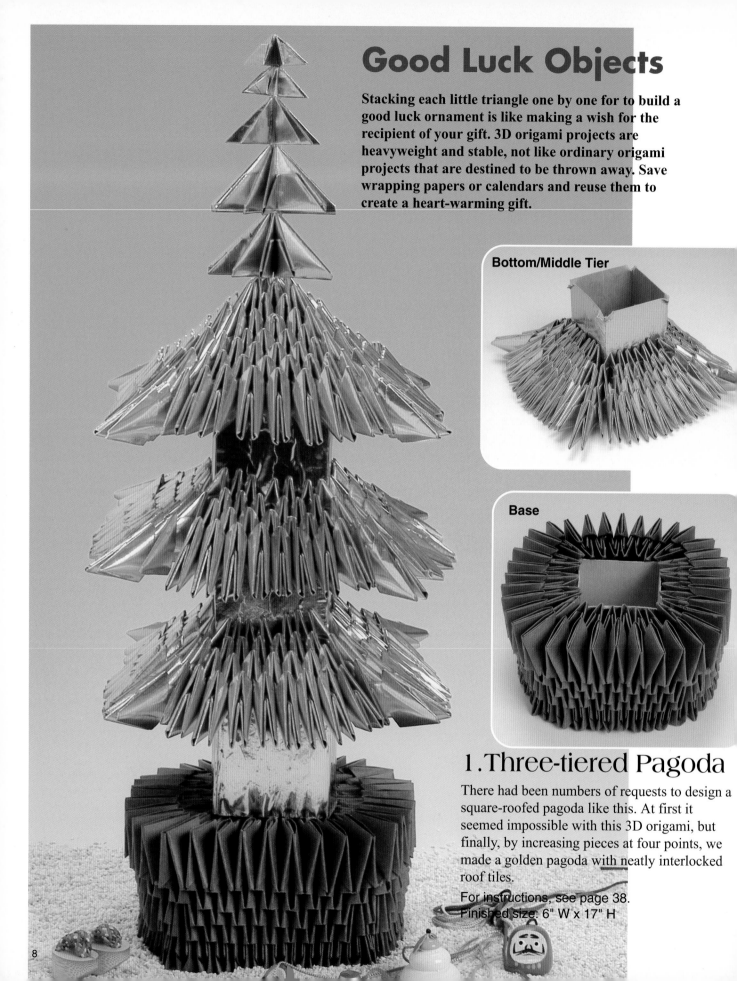

Bottom/Middle Tier

Base

1.Three-tiered Pagoda

There had been numbers of requests to design a square-roofed pagoda like this. At first it seemed impossible with this 3D origami, but finally, by increasing pieces at four points, we made a golden pagoda with neatly interlocked roof tiles.

For instructions, see page 38.
Finished size: 6" W x 17" H

2.Shogun Helmet

As a traditional decoration for Boys Day, this stately "metallic" helmet is a faithful copy of an antique kabuto or warrior's helmet.

For instructions, see page 42.
Finished size: 8" W x 10" H

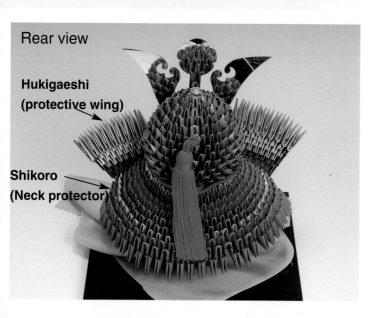

Rear view

Hukigaeshi (protective wing)

Shikoro (Neck protector)

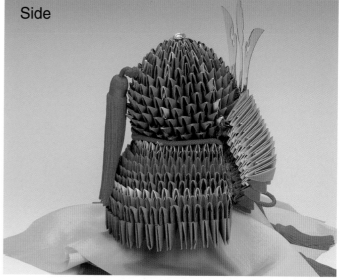

Side

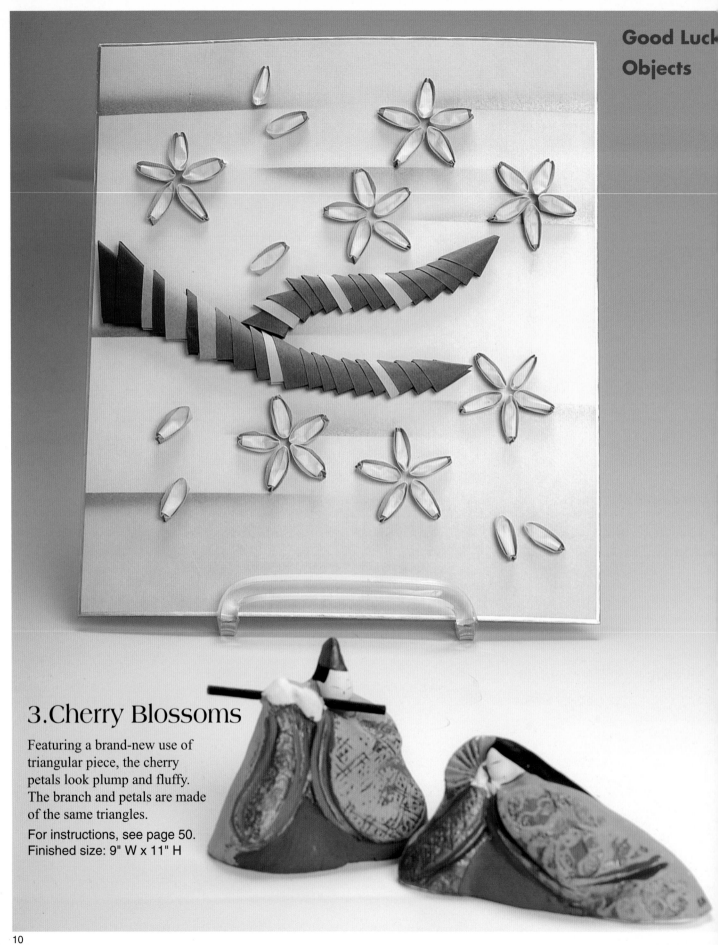

3.Cherry Blossoms

Featuring a brand-new use of
triangular piece, the cherry
petals look plump and fluffy.
The branch and petals are made
of the same triangles.

For instructions, see page 50.
Finished size: 9" W x 11" H

4.Mt. Fuji

An ideal project for beginners, this snow covered mountain requires flat assembly only.

For instructions, see page 54.
Finished size: 9" W x 11" H

5.Lucky Ball

A perfect ball was another challenging shape in 3D origami. Problems were solved: Begin with four pieces and increase in every row.

For instructions, see page 41. Finished size: $5\frac{1}{2}$" diameter

6.Seven Deities of Good Luck

For over 700 years these humorous deities have been a popular display among Japanese elder generations. Each deity, including a goddess, is said to bring happiness of each kind, as indicated in the parenthesis.

For instructions, see page 55-59. Finished size: 10" W x 6" H x 6 ½" D

Kotobuki(long life

Benzai(arts)

Hotei (abundance)

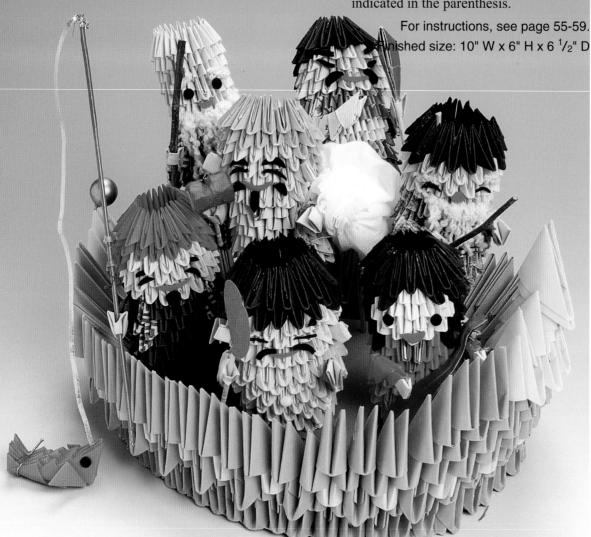

Fukurokuju (happiness)

Takarabune (Treasure boat)

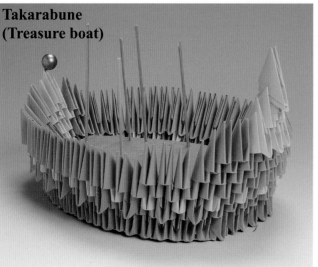

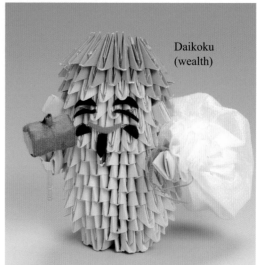

Daikoku (wealth)

7. Golden Age Couple

This loving couple has its roots in a famous Noh play called "Takasago." Dolls like these make a popular display as a symbol for longevity.

For instructions, see page 60 .
Finished size: 5" W x 2$\frac{1}{2}$" H

Bishamon(power)

Ebisu(integrity)

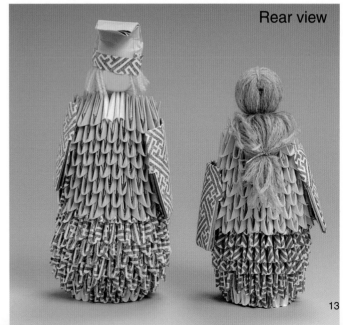

Rear view

13

Animal Symbols (Oriental Zodiac)

Make one figurine every year for your shelf, and have a set of twelve zodiac animals!

8.Mouse

A cute mouse emphasizing its big ears and head by using reverse assembly for the body.

For instructions, see page 62.
Finished size: 4" W x 5" H

Twelve zodiac animals are related to the date, the time of day, and the compass directions.

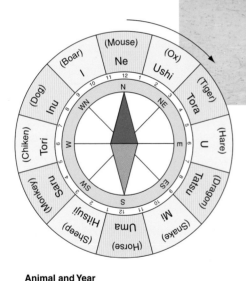

10.Tiger

Unique sitting tiger has pompon feet and "button" nose.

For instructions, see page 44.
Finished size: 9" W x 3 1/2" H

Animal and Year

Ne (Mouse)	1936	1948	1960	1972	1984	1996
Ushi (Ox)	37	49	61	73	85	97
Tora (Tiger)	38	50	62	74	86	98
U (Hare)	39	51	63	75	87	99
Tatsu (Dragon)	40	52	64	76	88	2000
Mi (Snake)	41	53	65	77	89	1
Uma (Horse)	42	54	66	78	90	2
Hitsuji (Sheep)	43	55	67	79	91	3
Saru (Monky)	44	56	68	80	92	4
Tori (Chiken)	45	57	69	81	93	5
Inu (Dog)	46	58	70	82	94	6
I (Boar)	47	59	71	83	95	7

The animal represents the year in which he/she was born.

9. Ox

Begin with a ring of triangles, and construct upward to make the body. Sitting ox bears a really heavyweight image.

For instructions, see page 64.
Finished size: 3" W x 4" H

Side

Rear view

11.Hare

Pale pink bunny has cocked up ears. Pair it
with smaller one made with smaller
triangles.

For instructions, see page 63.
Finished size: 3" W x 4" H

12.Dragon with Ball

The dragon is a symbol of lifting your fortune, just as it rises into the sky.

For instructions, see page 66.
Finished size: 1½" W x 7" H x 12" L

13.Dragon

Thinner than usual, this dragon is a reminiscence of unryu, or a dragon flying among clouds.

For instructions, see page 67.
Finished size: 1⅛" W x 2¼" H x 10" L

14.Snake

The scales are recreated by interlocking triangles in opposite direction alternately. Wire is inserted to shape the body.

For instructions, see page 67.
Finished size: 4" W x 6" H x 14" L

15. Horse (Pony)

This is a cute pony version, with oversized head. Make head, neck and body separately and assemble.

For instructions, see page 85.
Finished size: 2" W x 6" H

16. Sheep (Mother and Child)

The faces are made with Styrofoam ball wrapped in knitted fabric, and glued onto the body which is made easily.

For instructions, see page 70, 71.
Finished size: 4" W x 7" H (Mother)
3" W x 6" H (Child)

17.Sheep (Pair)

Construction begins with the back in order to express the voluminous fleece.

For instructions, see page 46.
Finished size: 3³⁄₄" W x 4¹⁄₄" H

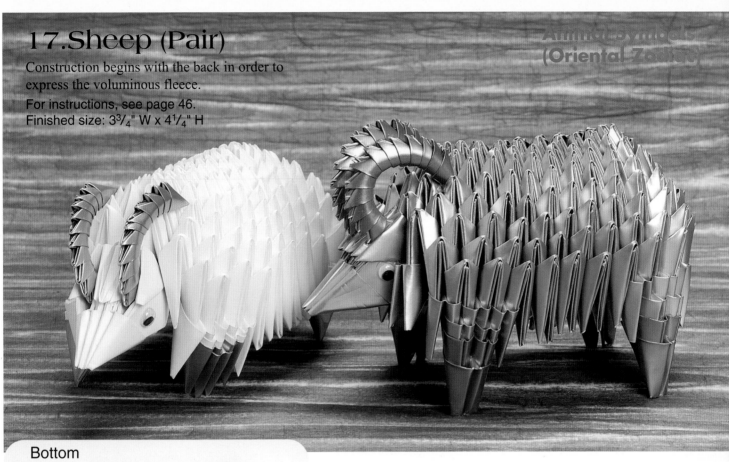

Bottom

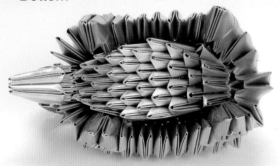

18.Sheep (Lamb)

This special iridescent paper does not make creases, which is ideal to create the fluffy fleece of baby sheep.

For instructions, see page 86.
Finished size: 2" W x 4" H

19.Monkey (Pair)

The thighs are attached after the body is done for the pursuit of reality. The colored part of the body represents vest.

For instructions, see page 68.
Finished size: 4¼" W x 6½" H

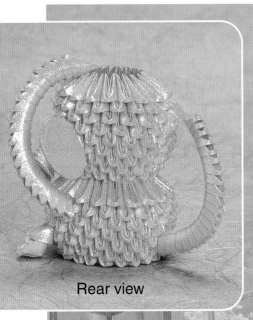

Rear view

20.Monkey (Girl)

Humorous, gibbon type monkey with long hands and tail, made of pink iridescent paper.

For instructions, see page 87.
Finished size: 2½" W x 4" H

21.Monkey
(Three Monkeys /See no evil, Speak no evil, Hear no evil)

Featuring the famous sculpture in Nikko, these monkeys represent the wish of their mother to stay away from evils in their childhood, or so they say. The limbs are long and free-moving.

For instructions, see page 76.   Finished size: 4" W x 5½" H (each)

22.Rooster (Satsuma)

Lean body and dignifying tail wing are a combination of different assembling methods.

For instructions, see page 52.
Finished size: 2¹/₄" W x 7" H

23.Chiken (Pair)

Looking as if on the point of pecking food, this plump pair will make you smile whenever you see them.

For instructions, see page 72 and 73.

Finished size: 2½" W x 6" H (Rooster)
2½" W x 4½" H (Hen)

24.Rooster (Parent and Child)

Birds are one of the most popular projects of origami. Focus on the proportion of neck and tail feathers.

For instructions, see page 88 and 89.

Finished size: 3" W x 4" H (Father)
1½" W x 2½" H (Child)

25.Dog

The coat looks as if combed through. Make a lovely feature by attaching muzzle and tongue.

For instructions, see page 74.
Finished size: 2" W x 5" H

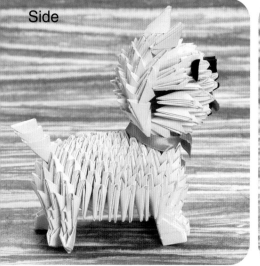
Side

Front

Bottom

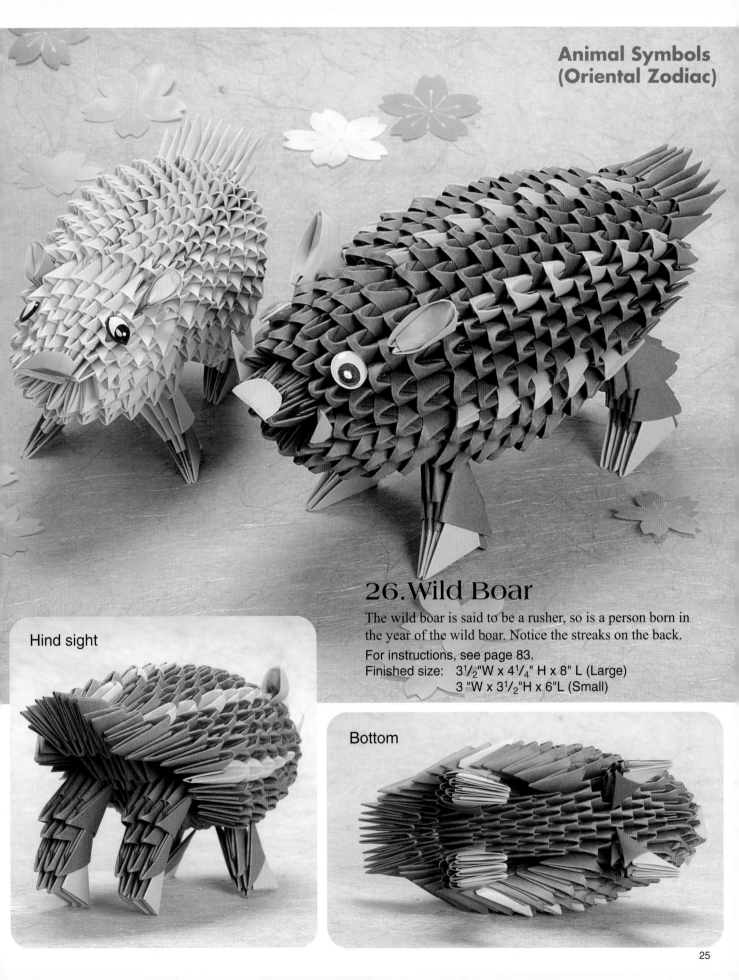

Hind sight

26. Wild Boar

The wild boar is said to be a rusher, so is a person born in the year of the wild boar. Notice the streaks on the back.

For instructions, see page 83.

Finished size: $3\frac{1}{2}$"W x $4\frac{1}{4}$" H x 8" L (Large)

3 "W x $3\frac{1}{2}$"H x 6"L (Small)

Bottom

Fancy Figures

Here are charming, dream-inspiring ornaments to be treasured for a long time.

27. Dragon Boat

Beautiful shiny boat will be a constant reminder of happy memories.

For instructions, see page 90.
Finished size: 3½" W x 4¼" H x 8" L

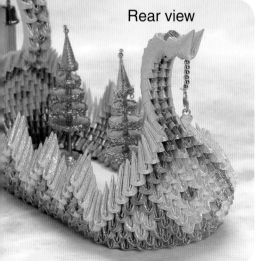

Rear view

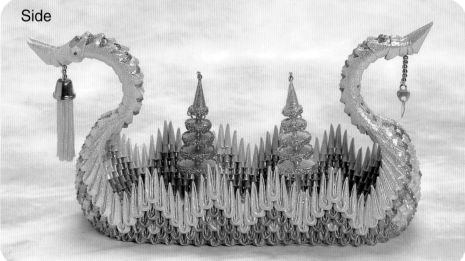

Side

28.Crane Basket

Flapping crane is made into such a lovely basket, in which you can arrange flowers, place candies, or potpourri.

For instructions, see page 92.
Finished size: 4½" W x 6" H

29.Basket

Shallow, diamond patterned basket has cardboard bottom for practical use.

For instructions, see page 93.
Finished size: 4½" W x 5" H

30.Peacock

Showing the distinctive patterns of tail feathers, these peacocks will invite you to the world of fairy tales.

For instructions, see page 48.
Finished size: 9" W x 10" H

Hind sight

Side

31.Brilliant Peacock

Enjoy the combination of colors as you increase the pieces for the tail feathers.

For instructions, see page 96.
Finished size: 5$\frac{1}{2}$" W x 4$\frac{1}{2}$" H

32.Penguin

The 3D origami triangle makes a perfect beak.

For instructions, see page 77.
Finished size: 4 " W x 6" H

Side

33.Feng Shui Kitty

The power of Feng Shui will increase when combined with popular Kitty.

For instructions, see page 78.
Finished size: 4¹/₂" W x 6" H

Feng Shui:

Literally, Feng means wind and Shui means water.

Ancient Chinese who lived in the old civilization regarded water as source of human life. They thought that the human was born from the water, raised by the water, and that the health and destiny were controlled by the water.

They also regarded strong wind as an angry sign of the God of Heaven, and believed the human destiny was controlled by the flow of the air. It was from such view of nature that the ancient Chinese cities were built where there are lot of water and less wind.

Feng Shui is also called the Chinese art of placement, and is used to promote well-being by bringing balance to one's home, body, business and relationships by creating a comfortable environment. It can be translated as "technologies utilizing the natural laws to create a comfortable life space."

34.Tulip

Two types of surface are made for tulips made from a small ring of triangles. The leaves are ma[de] of opened triangles glued together.

For instructions, see page 81.
Finished size: 2¹/₂ " W x 3" H

35.Squirrel

Put a nut between their hands? Instructions on page 94 are for the yellow squirrel, and the pink one has enlarged tail.

For instructions, see page 94.
Finished size: 2 " W x 3½" H

Hind sight

Side

36.Santa Claus

The thick black boots are constructed to stand the chubby old Santa.

For instructions, see page 80.
Finished size: 4 " W x 9" H

37.Snowman

Have fun attaching the details.

For instructions, see page 82.
Finished size: 3$\frac{1}{2}$" W x 7" H

38.Christmas Tree

Begin with 5 triangles for the top layer. You can make a larger tree with more pieces.

For instructions, see page 51.
Finished size: 4$\frac{1}{2}$" W x 8$\frac{1}{2}$" H

Hints for Gluing Pieces Together • • • • • • • • • • • • • •

● Securing 2-dimensional section or project

If you want the completed project to last longer, apply glue as you piece each triangle, or when necessary. However, we do not recommend use of glue when making your first project.

You need some experience to adjust the depth and angle of the insertion before locking up pieces.

For simple vertical insertion, apply a dab of glue onto double points.

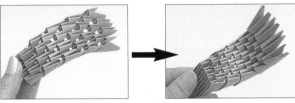

Apply glue onto the reverse side. Curl the whole to widen the surface for easy application. Be sure to align each row before the glue is dry.

To apply glue on the front side, loosen pieces beginning with the bottom row. Be sure to align each row before the glue is dry.

● Securing 3-dimensional section or project

Apply glue to the bottom row as you work. Do not glue pieces until each part is done and formed into shape. Use a bamboo skewer to place glue lightly onto one of the double pockets where pieces touch. Avoid deep insertion of the skewer as it may shift the piece when pulling it out, causing deformation of the project.

Otherwise, use a craft glue which has a narrow nozzle. It is easier to use, but consumes much more glue than applying with a skewer.

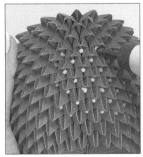

Use a narrow nozzle to apply glue from outside, under each piece.

Use a bamboo skewer to apply glue from outside under each piece.

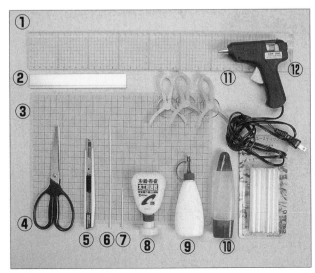

Utensils

① Long ruler (for cutting paper)
② Short ruler (for folding paper)
③ Cutting board
④ Scissors (for cutting paper)
⑤ Craft knife
⑥ Bamboo skewer
⑦ Wooden toothpick
⑧ Wood glue ⎫
⑨ Craft glue ⎬ (Use any type that turns clear when dried.)
⑩ Paper glue ⎭
⑪ Clothespins (for holding base ring)
⑫ Glue gun (for gluing smooth-faced paper such as gold-color paper)

Q&A

Q: How can I avoid unwanted center hole of the bottom?

A   This problem is caused by the bottom piecing and/or gluing. The size of the unwanted hole can be reduced by applying glue only to the tips. When the glue is applied to the middle of the pieces, it results in loose sections, causing unnecessary center hole.

   It also occurs when the triangles have too much ease. In this case, use triangles without extra easing for the bottom ring, and use eased triangles for the next row. This procedure will minimize the hole.

Loose piecing causes a large center hole.

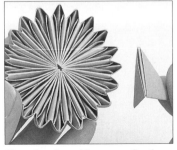

Use triangles without ease for the second row.

Q: The bottom pieces butt and stick out at the center!

A   This problem often occurs when working reverse assembly from the second row. One reason is that there are not enough easing on the adding triangles. Give a lot of ease especially for reverse assembly, and stack vertically.

   Another reason is that there are not enough number of pieces for the bottom. If you use less than 20 pieces for the bottom row, press the new pieces for the second row toward the center. Make the surface flat even if the center is twisted.

The center often sticks out when the second-row pieces are added in reverse direction.

Press down firmly so the center is fixed.

Q: The pieces come apart while making the bottom row!

A   Remember the following points:
● Do not stick more than 6 pieces at a time. If the pieces are too stiff to hold, stick 3-4 pieces together at one time.
● Secure the glued portions with clothespins until the glue is dried completely.
● When using clothespins to secure the glued portions into a ring, open the connecting triangles and press the adjacent pieces. Do not break the glued sections.

Apply glue only to the tips, not the middle.

Be sure not to break into glued sections.

Q: The pieces become irregular when assembled!

 It's natural that you tend to piece at an angle as long as you have your dominant hand.

To avoid this problem, change direction on every row, e.g. leftward on one row, then rightward on the next. You can also fix the directions of pieces after working every 2-3 rows.

The pieces look irregular.

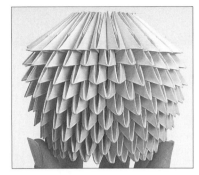

Alternate working direction on every row for a neat look.

Q: Reverse assembly is supposed to give flat or smooth surface, but I always end up with a "barrel" shape!

 That's because you set pieces at an angle. It's impossible to fix a part already glued, but if not glued yet, roll it on a flat surface back and forth until it becomes smooth, or press sides with your palms.

To keep the right shape, apply glue onto hidden points using a bamboo skewer.

A swollen cylinder

Press between your palms.

Q: Why do you need "ease" in the triangle?

 There are two reasons to add ease: One is to make it easy to open the pockets for easy insertion, and the other is to show the peaks neat and "prickly."

You can assemble pieces that are folded without ease, and the result is scale-like surface. Choose whichever type according to your aimed effects or your preference.

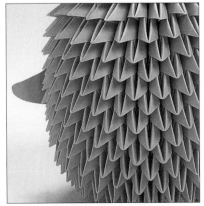

Pieces with ease

Pieces without ease

Q: How deep should the pieces are inserted?

 It is impossible to define how deep it must be since each person has different way of folding pieces. Just pay attention to create horizontal lines as you work each row. When the project is assembled, check the lines again before gluing together.

For a 2-dimensional project, smooth out the surface. It is a good idea to assemble rather loosely until 4 to 5 rows are made, and then adjust the shape and lines by pushing some pieces as necessary.

When all the pieces are interlocked, don't be afraid to press down the pieces or shape into an aimed form. Since pressing can cause irregular surfaces, it should be always followed by aligning the horizontal lines. By repeating this procedure, you will achieve the right shape.

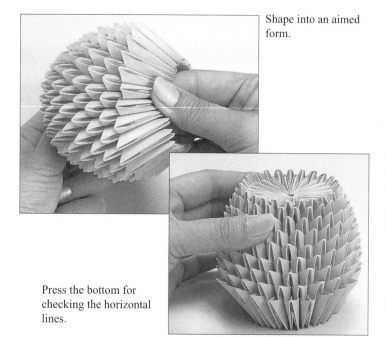

Shape into an aimed form.

Press the bottom for checking the horizontal lines.

Q: What's the knack to form a ball shape?

 Pay attention to piece angles of the ball surface as you stack a new piece, to form smooth outline. Also, always set the inner right-angles so they touch the previous right-angles closely. In other words, set the outer peaks so they stick out.

To adjust the shape after all the pieces are interlocked, press the pieces from inside with your thumbs so they form a perfect curve.

When all the pieces are interlocked, don't be afraid to press down the pieces or shape into a perfect form.

Since pressing can cause irregular surfaces, it should be always followed by aligning the horizontal lines. By repeating this procedure, you will achieve the right shape.

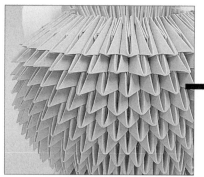
Outer peaks stick out.

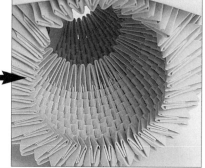
Inner surface is smooth.

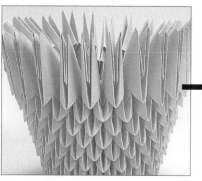
Outer peaks aline.

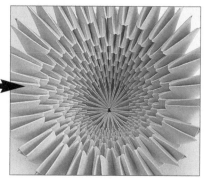
Inner peaks stick out.

Materials

617 1$\frac{1}{2}$" x 2$\frac{3}{4}$" rectangles*(gradated)

75 1$\frac{1}{2}$" x 2$\frac{3}{4}$" rectangles*(blue)

75 1$\frac{1}{2}$" x 2$\frac{3}{4}$" rectangles*(yellow)

1 $\frac{1}{2}$" x 2$\frac{3}{4}$" rectangles*(white)

1 $\frac{1}{2}$" square (skin) for hand

Fold rectangles* into triangles.

All rectangles* stand for pieces of paper to be folded into triangles. Prepare as many triangles as possible before actually assembling unless specified not to.

● Finished size (on gravure pages) is an approximate measurement. The completed size depends on each person's "hand."

▼ = blue

△▽ = red

▽· = yellow

▼ = white

The symbols indicate the colors and piecing directions.

From second row, the triangles are pointing downward. This is Regular Assembly.

The bottom row has triangles pointing upward. This means Reverse Assembly.

Papers for 3D Origami

On instruction pages, the paper materials are not specified as our previous books used to such as "origami paper" or "craft paper". This is to encourage you to choose any paper according to your imagination. Unlike traditional origami, this 3D craft calls for a certain stiffness, something between business envelope and ordinary origami paper. If using recycled paper, be sure to cut rectangles of a certain ratio for the main parts. Remember that the final project is not affected by the ratio of the basic rectangles.

Most projects introduced in this book are made from commercial paper sold as origami craft paper, in a variety of precut sizes including 1$\frac{1}{2}$" x 2$\frac{3}{4}$", 2" x 3$\frac{1}{2}$", 2$\frac{1}{2}$" x 4$\frac{1}{4}$" or 2$\frac{3}{4}$" x 5" rectangles. As 3D Origami has been popular for nearly a decade, even miniature sized commercial rectangles such as 1" x 2" are in the market today.

Practice makes perfect!

Assembly

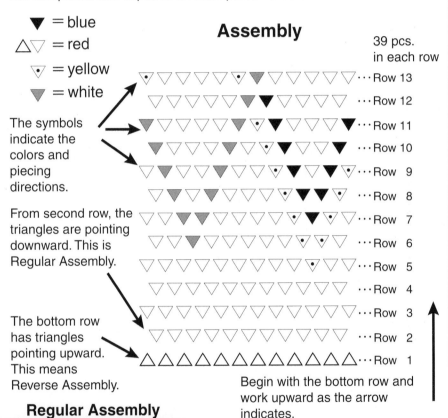

39 pcs. in each row

··· Row 13
··· Row 12
··· Row 11
··· Row 10
··· Row 9
··· Row 8
··· Row 7
··· Row 6
··· Row 5
··· Row 4
··· Row 3
··· Row 2
··· Row 1

Begin with the bottom row and work upward as the arrow indicates.

Regular Assembly

Reverse Assembly

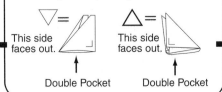

Signs for piecing direction

▽ = This side faces out. / Double Pocket

△ = This side faces out. / Double Pocket

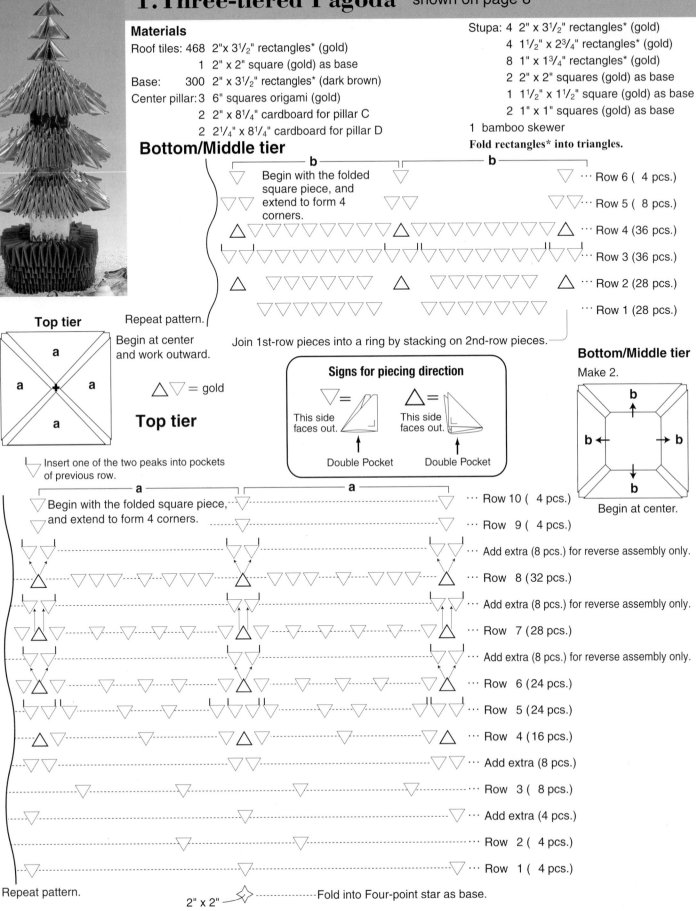

1. Three-tiered Pagoda shown on page 8

Materials

Roof tiles: 468 2" x 3½" rectangles* (gold)
1 2" x 2" square (gold) as base
Base: 300 2" x 3½" rectangles* (dark brown)
Center pillar: 3 6" squares origami (gold)
2 2" x 8¼" cardboard for pillar C
2 2¼" x 8¼" cardboard for pillar D

Stupa: 4 2" x 3½" rectangles* (gold)
4 1½" x 2¾" rectangles* (gold)
8 1" x 1¾" rectangles* (gold)
2 2" x 2" squares (gold) as base
1 1½" x 1½" square (gold) as base
2 1" x 1" squares (gold) as base

1 bamboo skewer

Fold rectangles* into triangles.

Bottom/Middle tier

Begin with the folded square piece, and extend to form 4 corners.

··· Row 6 (4 pcs.)
··· Row 5 (8 pcs.)
··· Row 4 (36 pcs.)
··· Row 3 (36 pcs.)
··· Row 2 (28 pcs.)
··· Row 1 (28 pcs.)

Join 1st-row pieces into a ring by stacking on 2nd-row pieces.

Repeat pattern.

Top tier

Begin at center and work outward.

△▽ = gold

Begin with the folded square piece, and extend to form 4 corners.

Insert one of the two peaks into pockets of previous row.

Signs for piecing direction

▽ = This side faces out. Double Pocket
△ = This side faces out. Double Pocket

Bottom/Middle tier

Make 2.

Begin at center.

··· Row 10 (4 pcs.)
··· Row 9 (4 pcs.)
··· Add extra (8 pcs.) for reverse assembly only.
··· Row 8 (32 pcs.)
··· Add extra (8 pcs.) for reverse assembly only.
··· Row 7 (28 pcs.)
··· Add extra (8 pcs.) for reverse assembly only.
··· Row 6 (24 pcs.)
··· Row 5 (24 pcs.)
··· Row 4 (16 pcs.)
··· Add extra (8 pcs.)
··· Row 3 (8 pcs.)
··· Add extra (4 pcs.)
··· Row 2 (4 pcs.)
··· Row 1 (4 pcs.)

Repeat pattern.

2" x 2" Fold into Four-point star as base.

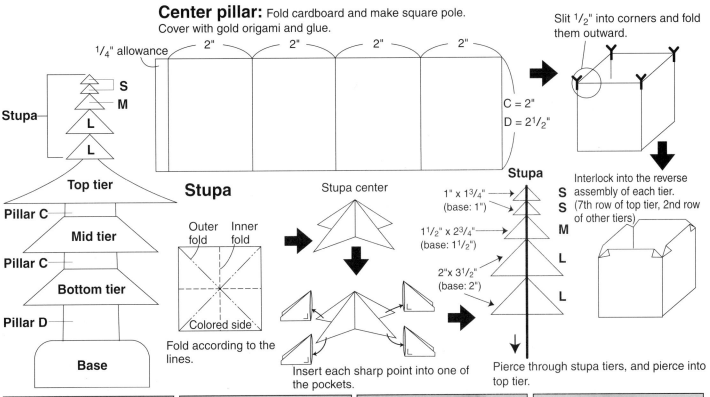

Center pillar: Fold cardboard and make square pole. Cover with gold origami and glue.

1/4" allowance

2" 2" 2" 2"

Slit 1/2" into corners and fold them outward.

C = 2"
D = 2 1/2"

Interlock into the reverse assembly of each tier. (7th row of top tier, 2nd row of other tiers)

Stupa

S
M
L
L

Top tier
Pillar C
Mid tier
Pillar C
Bottom tier
Pillar D
Base

Stupa

Stupa center

Outer fold   Inner fold

Colored side

Fold according to the lines.

Insert each sharp point into one of the pockets.

Stupa

1" x 1 3/4" (base: 1")   S
                         S
1 1/2" x 2 3/4" (base: 1 1/2")   M
                                  L
2" x 3 1/2" (base: 2")   L

Pierce through stupa tiers, and pierce into top tier.

Top tier

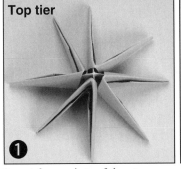

❶ Insert four points of the stupa tier into one each pocket of 4 triangles. This makes Row 1.

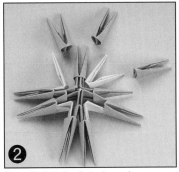

❷ Row 2: Interlock 4 pieces by inserting 2 adjacent peaks of Row 1 into each. Row 3: Add 4 half-open pieces to the space, and interlock them with adjacent peaks using 8 new pieces.

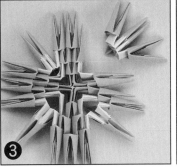

❸ Row 4: Adding 2 pieces evenly to 4 spaces, interlock them with the pieces of Row 3, using 16 pieces. In the same manner, continue increasing pieces referring to the chart (opposite).

Bottom/Middle tier

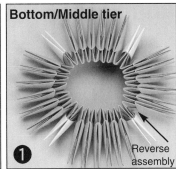

❶ Join pieces of Row 1 by inserting them into the pockets of Row 2 pieces, reversing direction of the new piece at 4 corners. (Added pieces are shown in different color for easy comprehension.)

Reverse assembly

Row 3: Work Row 3 by interlocking with 36 pieces, adding 2 pieces at the reverse assembly to make 4 corners.

Row 4: Add one piece to each corner in reverse assembly as you interlock 36 pieces all around.

Shape inner square hole by temporarily setting the pillar (the golden paper not yet glued on).

Showing the backside. Check if the corners stick out, touching the adjacent regular pieces.

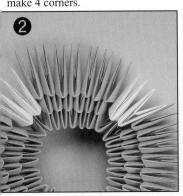

❷

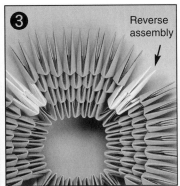

❸ Reverse assembly

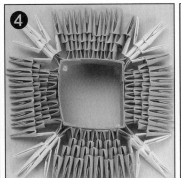

❹

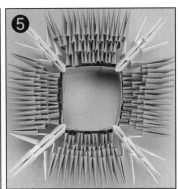

❺

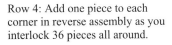

1. Three-tiered Pagoda shown on page 8

Base

Finished size:
5" W x 2 ½" H (approx.)

Begin with a ring, and
shape into square.

Place a cardboard pillar
for shaping.

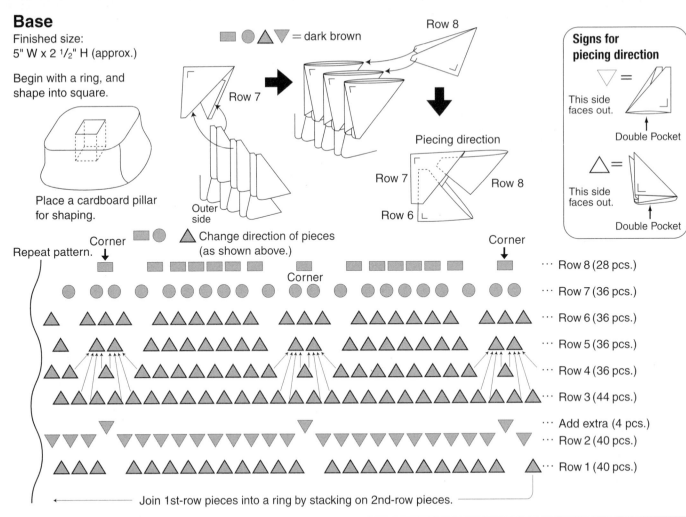

◼ ● ▲ ▼ = dark brown

Row 8

Row 7

Outer
side

Piecing direction

Row 7   Row 8

Row 6

Signs for piecing direction

▽ =
This side faces out.
Double Pocket

△ =
This side faces out.
Double Pocket

Repeat pattern.

Corner

◼ ●   ▲ Change direction of pieces
(as shown above.)

Corner

Corner

··· Row 8 (28 pcs.)

··· Row 7 (36 pcs.)

··· Row 6 (36 pcs.)

··· Row 5 (36 pcs.)

··· Row 4 (36 pcs.)

··· Row 3 (44 pcs.)

··· Add extra (4 pcs.)

··· Row 2 (40 pcs.)

··· Row 1 (40 pcs.)

← Join 1st-row pieces into a ring by stacking on 2nd-row pieces. →

Backside of Base

Top of Base

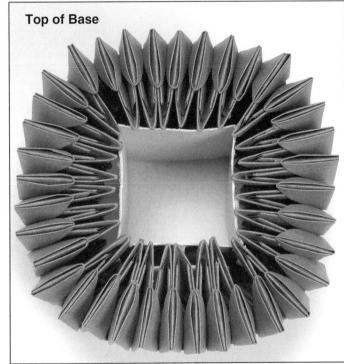

5. Lucky Ball shown on page 11

Materials
156 1½" x 3" rectangles*(gold)
36 1½" x 3" rectangles* each in red, blue, light green, navy, yellow, orange, green, pink
1 1½" x 1½" square (gold) as base
1 fringed cording (red)
Fold rectangles* into triangles.

Note: Be sure to position gold pieces to form whirling streaks. Change color between the golden streaks.

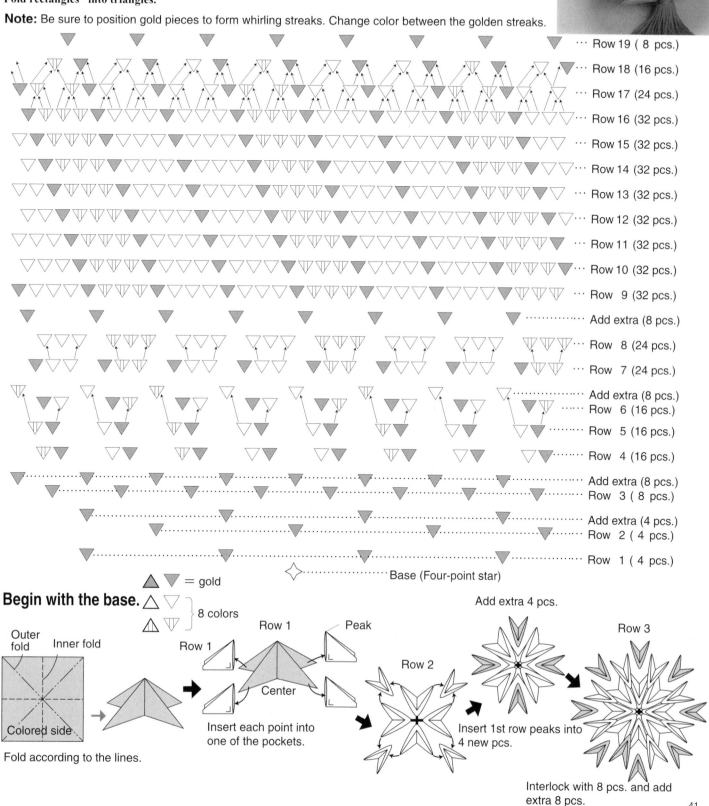

··· Row 19 (8 pcs.)
··· Row 18 (16 pcs.)
··· Row 17 (24 pcs.)
··· Row 16 (32 pcs.)
··· Row 15 (32 pcs.)
··· Row 14 (32 pcs.)
··· Row 13 (32 pcs.)
··· Row 12 (32 pcs.)
··· Row 11 (32 pcs.)
··· Row 10 (32 pcs.)
··· Row 9 (32 pcs.)
············ Add extra (8 pcs.)
··· Row 8 (24 pcs.)
··· Row 7 (24 pcs.)
············ Add extra (8 pcs.)
············ Row 6 (16 pcs.)
··· Row 5 (16 pcs.)
······· Row 4 (16 pcs.)
············ Add extra (8 pcs.)
············ Row 3 (8 pcs.)
Add extra (4 pcs.)
Row 2 (4 pcs.)
Row 1 (4 pcs.)

Base (Four-point star)

△ ▽ = gold

Begin with the base. △ ▽ } 8 colors
△ ▽

Outer fold   Inner fold

Colored side

Fold according to the lines.

Row 1   Peak
Row 1
Center
Insert each point into one of the pockets.

Row 2
Insert 1st row peaks into 4 new pcs.

Add extra 4 pcs.

Row 3
Interlock with 8 pcs. and add extra 8 pcs.

41

2.Shogun Helmet shown on page 9

Materials for Brown Helmet

415 1½" x 3" rectangles* (black)
150 1½" x 3" rectangles* (gold)
102 1½" x 3" rectangles* (red)
 30 1½" x 3" rectangles* (silver)
  2 1½" x 1½" squares (green) as base
  1 7" x 4" stiff paper (gold) for crest

1 acrylic decorative ornament
6 crest-shaped spangles
4"L large fringe (red)
3 ft. fringed fabric cording (red)
Fold rectangles* into triangles.

Note: Make 4 parts separately and put them together with glue gun.

Neck protector

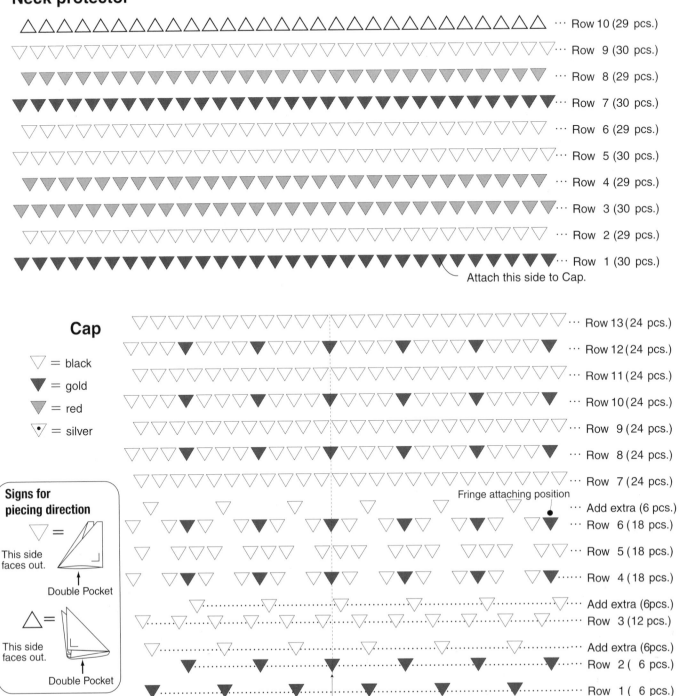

Row 10 (29 pcs.)
Row 9 (30 pcs.)
Row 8 (29 pcs.)
Row 7 (30 pcs.)
Row 6 (29 pcs.)
Row 5 (30 pcs.)
Row 4 (29 pcs.)
Row 3 (30 pcs.)
Row 2 (29 pcs.)
Row 1 (30 pcs.)
Attach this side to Cap.

Cap

▽ = black
▼ = gold
▼ = red
▼• = silver

Row 13 (24 pcs.)
Row 12 (24 pcs.)
Row 11 (24 pcs.)
Row 10 (24 pcs.)
Row 9 (24 pcs.)
Row 8 (24 pcs.)
Row 7 (24 pcs.)

Fringe attaching position
Add extra (6 pcs.)
Row 6 (18 pcs.)
Row 5 (18 pcs.)
Row 4 (18 pcs.)
Add extra (6pcs.)
Row 3 (12 pcs.)
Add extra (6pcs.)
Row 2 (6 pcs.)
Row 1 (6 pcs.)

Center Front
2 pcs. 1½" squares
Base (Six-point star)

Signs for piecing direction

▽ =
This side faces out.
↑ Double Pocket

△ =
This side faces out.
↑ Double Pocket

42

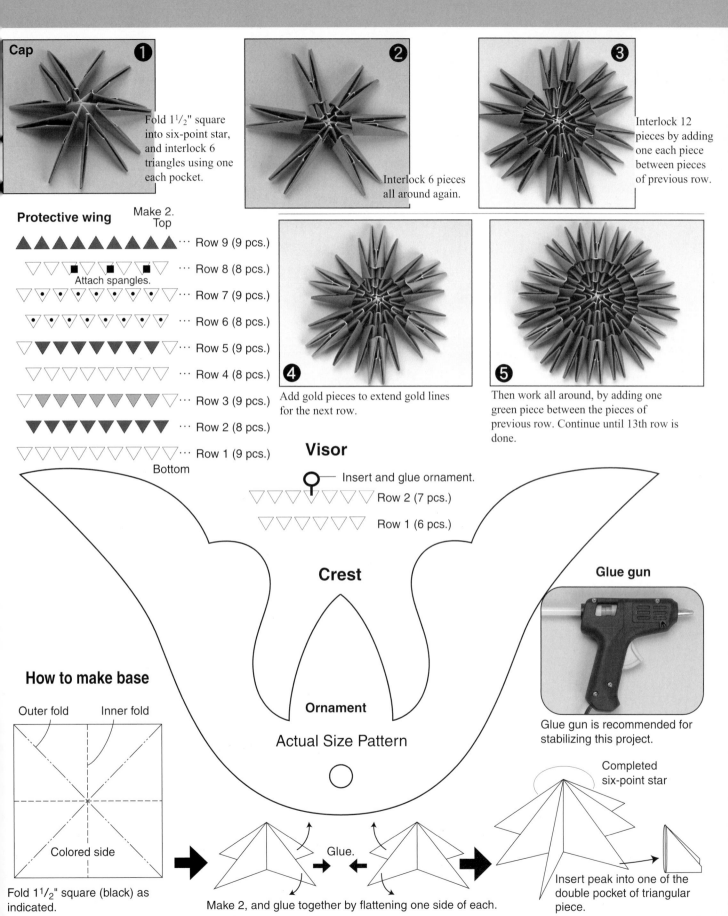

Cap

① Fold 1 1/2" square into six-point star, and interlock 6 triangles using one each pocket.

② Interlock 6 pieces all around again.

③ Interlock 12 pieces by adding one each piece between pieces of previous row.

④ Add gold pieces to extend gold lines for the next row.

⑤ Then work all around, by adding one green piece between the pieces of previous row. Continue until 13th row is done.

Protective wing

Make 2.
Top

··· Row 9 (9 pcs.)

··· Row 8 (8 pcs.)
Attach spangles.

··· Row 7 (9 pcs.)

··· Row 6 (8 pcs.)

··· Row 5 (9 pcs.)

··· Row 4 (8 pcs.)

··· Row 3 (9 pcs.)

··· Row 2 (8 pcs.)

··· Row 1 (9 pcs.)
Bottom

Visor

— Insert and glue ornament.
Row 2 (7 pcs.)

Row 1 (6 pcs.)

Crest

Ornament

Actual Size Pattern

Glue gun

Glue gun is recommended for stabilizing this project.

How to make base

Outer fold   Inner fold

Colored side

Fold 1 1/2" square (black) as indicated.

Make 2, and glue together by flattening one side of each.

Glue.

Completed six-point star

Insert peak into one of the double pocket of triangular piece.

10. Tiger shown on page 14

Materials

520 1 1/2" x 2 3/4" rectangles* (yellow)
100 1 1/2" x 2 3/4" rectangles* (black)
98 1 1/2" x 2 3/4" rectangles* (white)
1 1 1/4" x 1 1/4" square (yellow) as base

1 3/8" button for nose
6 4" nylon string pieces for whiskers
2 1/2" pompons for feet
Fold rectangles* into triangles.

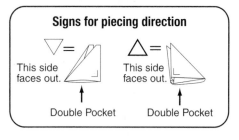

Signs for piecing direction

▽ =
This side faces out.
Double Pocket

△ =
This side faces out.
Double Pocket

Head

❸
Row 3: Adding 4 black pieces evenly between previous pieces, interlock them with 8 pieces.

❶
Row 1: Insert four points of base into 4 triangular pieces.

Ear Make 2.

△ △ ⋯ Row 4 (2 pcs.)
△ △ △ ⋯ Row 3 (3 pcs.)
△ △ △ △ ⋯ Row 2 (4 pcs.)
△ △ △ △ △ ⋯ Row 1 (5 pcs.)

Insert short-cut toothpick here.

△ ▽ = yellow
▲ ▼ = black
△• ▽• = white

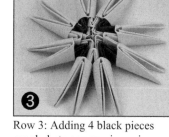

❷
Row 2: Stack on 4 pieces again.

Head

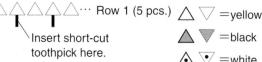

Center Front

⋯ Row 18 (4 pcs.)
⋯ Row 17 (10 pcs.)
⋯ Row 16 (13 pcs.)
⋯ Row 15 (14 pcs.)
⋯ Row 14 (17 pcs.)
⋯ Row 13 (18 pcs.)
⋯ Row 12 (20 pcs.)
⋯ Row 11 (20 pcs.)
⋯ Row 10 (20 pcs.)
⋯ Row 9 (20 pcs.)

Ear attaching position

⋯ Row 8 (20 pcs.)
⋯ Row 7 (20 pcs.)
⋯ Row 6 (20 pcs.)
⋯ Row 5 (20 pcs.)

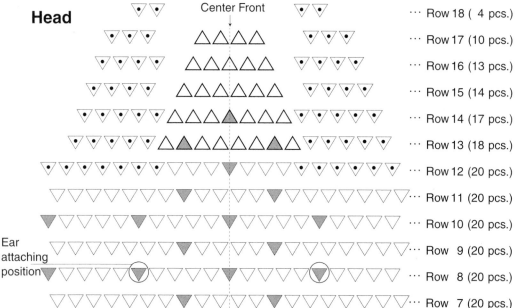

⋯ Add extra (8 pcs.)
⋯ Row 4 (12 pcs.)

⋯ Add extra (4 pcs.)
⋯ Row 3 (8 pcs.)

⋯ Add extra (4 pcs.)
⋯ Row 2 (4 pcs.)

⋯ Row 1 (4 pcs.)

⟡ ⋯⋯⋯⋯⋯ Base (Four-point star)

❹
Row 4: In order to form stripes, interlock 4 black pieces first.

5 Adding extra 4 yellow pieces evenly, interlock them with remaining 8 yellow pieces.

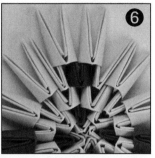

6 Row 5: Adding 8 extra pieces evenly to both sides of the black pieces, interlock 20 pieces.

7 Row 5 is worked all around.

8 Showing when Row 11 is completed. At this point secure pieces with glue since they may slip off easily.

9 Row 12-18: Continue assembling in the same manner, changing colors according to the figure on opposite page. Work the face portion in reverse assembly, and decrease pieces for chin.

Tail

Insert into body.

▽ ··· Row 23
▽ ··· Row 22
▼ ··· Row 21
▽ ··· Row 20
▽ ··· Row 19
▼ ··· Row 18

Use black pcs. on Rows 9,12 and 15. Use yellow on remaining rows.

▽ ··· Row 8
▽ ··· Row 7
▼ ··· Row 6
▽ ··· Row 5
▽ ··· Row 4
▼ ··· Row 3
▽• ··· Row 2
▽• ··· Row 1

Hand   Make 2.

▽ ▽ ··· Row 13 (2 pcs.)
▽ ▽ ▽ ··· Row 12 (3 pcs.)
▽ ▽ ··· Row 11 (2 pcs.)
▽ ▽ ▽ ··· Row 10 (3 pcs.)
▼ ▼ ··· Row 9 (2 pcs.)
▽ ▽ ▽ ··· Row 8 (3 pcs.)
▽ ▽ ··· Row 7 (2 pcs.)
▽ ▽ ▽ ··· Row 6 (3 pcs.)
▼ ▼ ··· Row 5 (2 pcs.)
▽ ▽ ▽ ··· Row 4 (3 pcs.)
▽ ▽ ··· Row 3 (2 pcs.)
▽• ▽ ▽• ··· Row 2 (3 pcs.)
▽• ▽• ··· Row 1 (2 pcs.)

Leg   Make 2.

Insert into body.

▽ ▽ ··· Row 5 (2 pcs.)
▽ ··· Row 4 (3 pcs.)
▼ ▼ ··· Row 3 (2 pcs.)
▽ ··· Row 2 (3 pcs.)
▽ ▽ ··· Row 1 (2 pcs.)
◯ ←Glue on pompon.

Eyes

Actual Size Pattern

△ ▽ = yellow
▲ ▼ = black
△• ▽• = white

Body

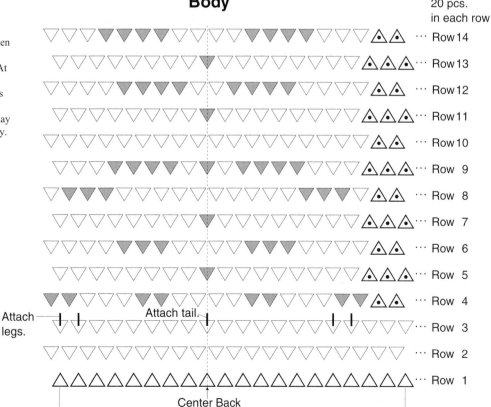

20 pcs. in each row

Row 14
Row 13
Row 12
Row 11
Row 10
Row 9
Row 8
Row 7
Row 6
Row 5
Row 4
Row 3 — Attach legs. / Attach tail.
Row 2
Row 1

Center Back
Join 20 pieces in a ring.

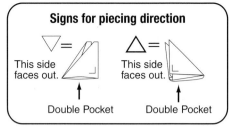

17. Sheep shown on page 19

Materials for White Sheep

- 245 2" x 4¼" rectangles* (white)
- 12 2" x 4¼" rectangles* (silver) for limbs
- 12 2" x 3½" rectangles* (white) for head
- 28 1" x 2¼" rectangles* (silver) for horns
- 20 2" x 2" squares (white) as base
- 2 ¼" plastic joggle eyes

Fold rectangles* into triangles.

△ ▽ = white
△ ▽ = silver

Row 1

Row 1 pc.   Row 1 pc.

2 base pcs. are encased.

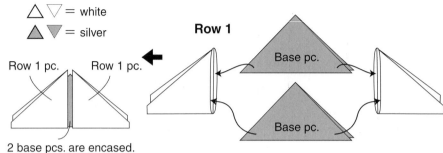

Base pc.
Base pc.

Row 2

Row 2 pc.   Row 2 pc.

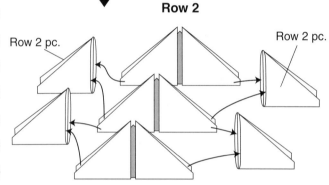

Belly

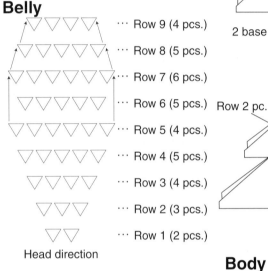

- ··· Row 9 (4 pcs.)
- ··· Row 8 (5 pcs.)
- ··· Row 7 (6 pcs.)
- ··· Row 6 (5 pcs.)
- ··· Row 5 (4 pcs.)
- ··· Row 4 (5 pcs.)
- ··· Row 3 (4 pcs.)
- ··· Row 2 (3 pcs.)
- ··· Row 1 (2 pcs.)

Head direction

Base (backbone)

Use 2" square.

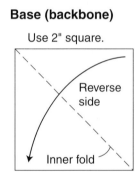

Reverse side

Inner fold

Inner fold

Make 20.

Body

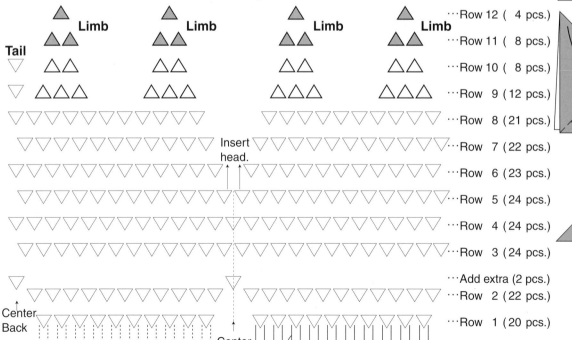

Tail   Limb   Limb   Limb   Limb

- ···Row 12 (4 pcs.)
- ···Row 11 (8 pcs.)
- ···Row 10 (8 pcs.)
- ···Row 9 (12 pcs.)
- ···Row 8 (21 pcs.)

Insert head.

- ···Row 7 (22 pcs.)
- ···Row 6 (23 pcs.)
- ···Row 5 (24 pcs.)
- ···Row 4 (24 pcs.)
- ···Row 3 (24 pcs.)
- ···Add extra (2 pcs.)
- ···Row 2 (22 pcs.)
- ···Row 1 (20 pcs.)

Center Back

Center

Base pieces form backbone of sheep (20 pcs.)

Form backbone on Rows 1- 2.

Top view

Add.

Row 2

Row 1

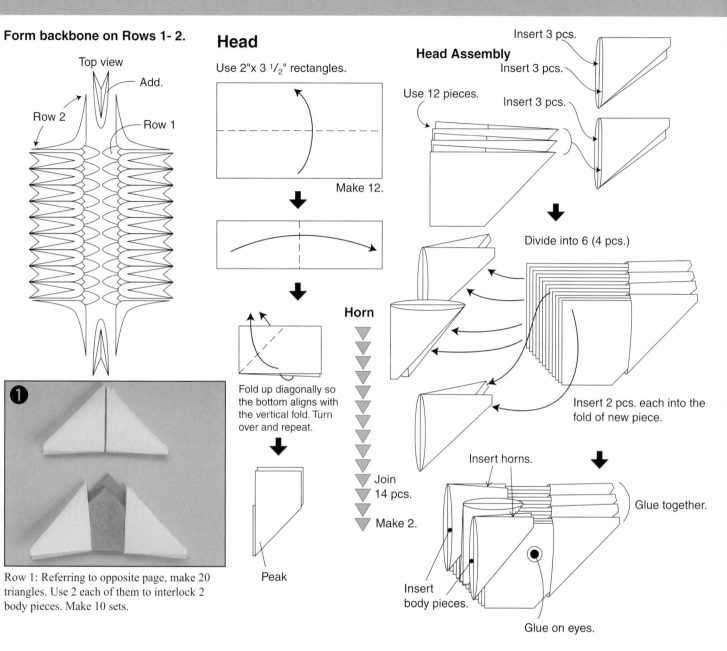

❶

Row 1: Referring to opposite page, make 20 triangles. Use 2 each of them to interlock 2 body pieces. Make 10 sets.

Head

Use 2"x 3 ½" rectangles.

Make 12.

Fold up diagonally so the bottom aligns with the vertical fold. Turn over and repeat.

Peak

Horn

Join
14 pcs.

Make 2.

Head Assembly

Insert 3 pcs.

Insert 3 pcs.

Use 12 pieces.

Insert 3 pcs.

Divide into 6 (4 pcs.)

Insert 2 pcs. each into the fold of new piece.

Insert horns.

Glue together.

Insert body pieces.

Glue on eyes.

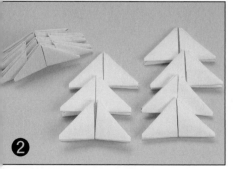

❷

Row 2: Insert both sides of Row-1 pieces to new Row-2 pieces so the separate units are joined into a straight backbone.

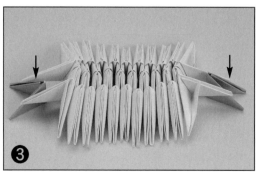

❸

After adding 10 pieces to each side, place 1 extra piece to both ends.

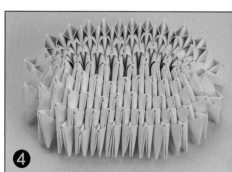

❹

Row 3-4: Adding these extra, work all around interlocking adjacent peaks of previous row with new pieces. When 4th row is done, the rounded body begins to form. Continue as indicated in the chart.

30.Peacock shown on page 28

Materials for Pink Peacock

567 1¼" x 2¼" rectangles* (pink)
320 1¼" x 2¼" rectangles* (white)
119 1¼" x 2¼" rectangles* (gold)
 27 1¼" x 2¼" rectangles* (green)
 27 1¼" x 2¼" rectangles* (red)
  2 ¼" plastic joggle eyes
  3 pearl-head marking pins

Fold rectangles* into triangles.

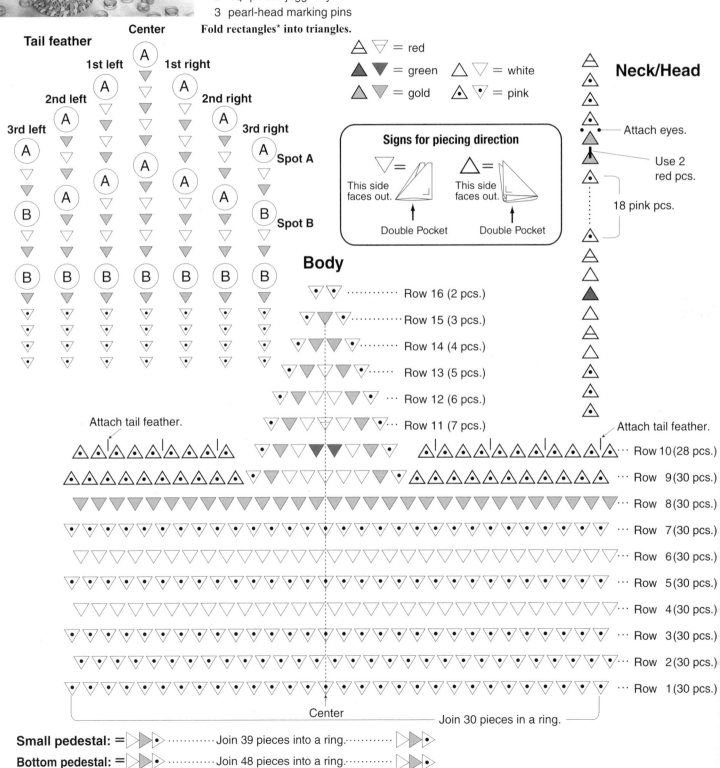

Tail feather

Center

1st left 1st right

2nd left 2nd right

3rd left 3rd right

Spot A

Spot B

= red
= green   = white
= gold   = pink

Signs for piecing direction

This side faces out.   This side faces out.

Double Pocket   Double Pocket

Neck/Head

Attach eyes.

Use 2 red pcs.

18 pink pcs.

Body

Row 16 (2 pcs.)
Row 15 (3 pcs.)
Row 14 (4 pcs.)
Row 13 (5 pcs.)
Row 12 (6 pcs.)
Row 11 (7 pcs.)

Attach tail feather.   Attach tail feather.

Row 10 (28 pcs.)
Row 9 (30 pcs.)
Row 8 (30 pcs.)
Row 7 (30 pcs.)
Row 6 (30 pcs.)
Row 5 (30 pcs.)
Row 4 (30 pcs.)
Row 3 (30 pcs.)
Row 2 (30 pcs.)
Row 1 (30 pcs.)

Center   Join 30 pieces in a ring.

Small pedestal: = ▷▷▷▸ ·········· Join 39 pieces into a ring ·········· ▷▷▷▸
Bottom pedestal: = ▷▷▷▸ ·········· Join 48 pieces into a ring ·········· ▷▷▷▸

Center

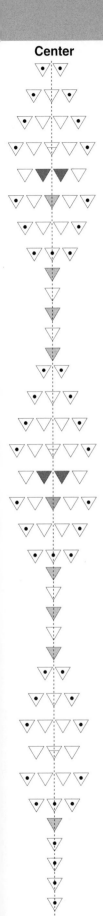

1st right
1st left

Wing

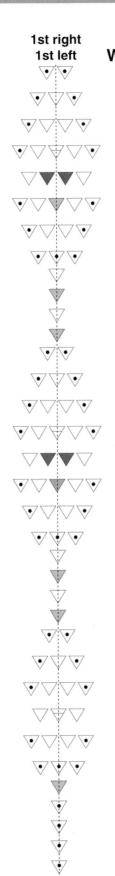

2nd right
2nd left

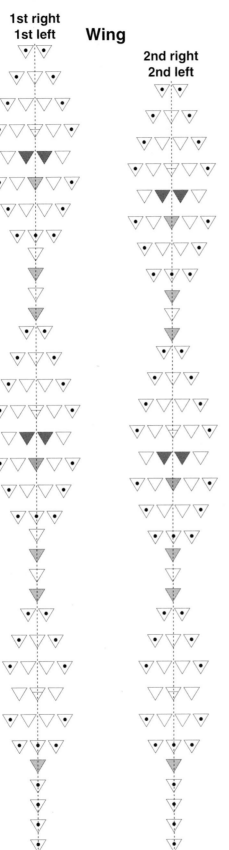

3rd right
3rd left

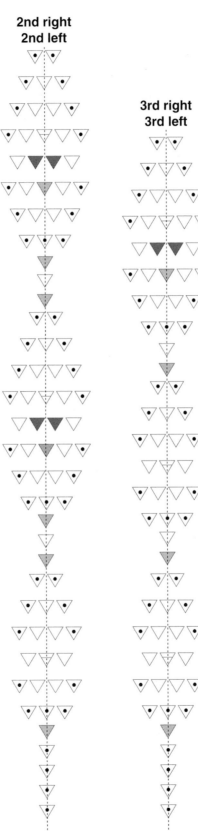

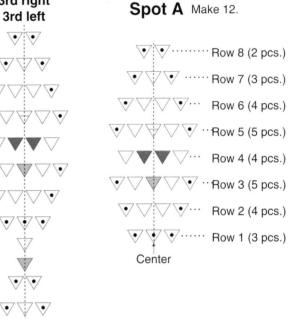

△ ▽ = red △ ▽ = white
▲ ▼ = green △ ▼ = yellow
△ ▼ = gold

Spot A Make 12.

Row 8 (2 pcs.)
Row 7 (3 pcs.)
Row 6 (4 pcs.)
Row 5 (5 pcs.)
Row 4 (4 pcs.)
Row 3 (5 pcs.)
Row 2 (4 pcs.)
Row 1 (3 pcs.)

Center

Spot B Make 9.

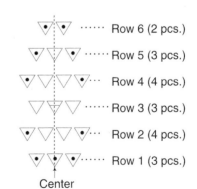

Row 6 (2 pcs.)
Row 5 (3 pcs.)
Row 4 (4 pcs.)
Row 3 (3 pcs.)
Row 2 (4 pcs.)
Row 1 (3 pcs.)

Center

3. Cherry Blossoms shown on page 10

Materials

Blossoms:
42 $1^1/_2$" x $2^3/_4$" rectangles* (gradated pink)

Branch:
20 $1^1/_2$" x $2^3/_4$" rectangles* (dark brown)
4 $1^1/_2$" x $2^3/_4$" rectangles* (light brown)
4 2" x $3^1/_2$" rectangles* (dark brown)
1 2" x $3^1/_2$" rectangle* (light brown)

2 $2^1/_2$" x $4^1/_4$" rectangles* (dark brown)
3 $2^1/_2$" x $4^1/_4$" rectangles* (light brown)
2 3" x 6" rectangles* (dark brown)
1 10" x 11" Shikishi (large square writing card)
Carving chisel
Toothpick
Cotton-tipped swab
Fold rectangles* into triangles.

Signs for piecing direction

$\triangledown$ = This side faces out. ↑ Double Pocket

$\triangle$ = This side faces out. ↑ Double Pocket

$\triangle$ = light brown
▲ = dark brown

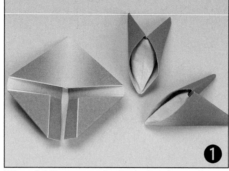

① When folding rectangles into triangles, make sure to give a lot of ease, and also to show pale pink shade in pockets.

④ Insert petal pieces so the peaks of 5 pieces scarcely touch at the center.

Long branch   Short branch

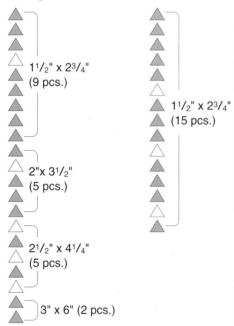

Long branch:
$1^1/_2$" x $2^3/_4$" (9 pcs.)
2" x $3^1/_2$" (5 pcs.)
$2^1/_2$" x $4^1/_4$" (5 pcs.)
3" x 6" (2 pcs.)

Short branch:
$1^1/_2$" x $2^3/_4$" (15 pcs.)

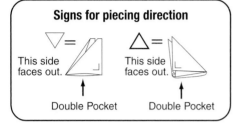

② Make branches as indicated left. Trace the blossom pattern with a piece of paper, and make 5 incisions. Position branches on card, and mark incisions with a pencil where blossoms should be placed.

⑤ Turn over the card. Open out the triangles that are sticking out. No gluing is necessary as they will stay securely.

Blossom pattern

Make incisions along thick lines.

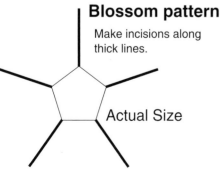

Actual Size

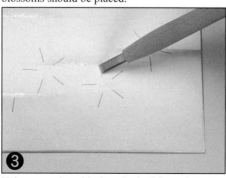

③ Using a carving chisel, make incisions along the lines deep enough to insert blossoms.

⑥ Turn over again, and press open the pockets. To avoid too much pressure, insert a toothpick through center of petal, and press down gently with a cotton-tip swab.

38.Christmas Tree   shown on page 32

Attach gold star.

A
B
C
D
E

Insert bamboo skewer through tiers.

Pot ···
Styrofoam

Tier

Materials

180 2"x 3½" rectangles* (green)
100 2"x 3½" rectangles* (brown)
  2 1" x 1" square (gold) for tree top
1 long bamboo skewer
Styrofoam block
Ornaments (ribbon bows, pompons, fake snow, etc.)
Fold rectangles* into triangles.

Row 5
Row 4
L

20 pcs. in each row

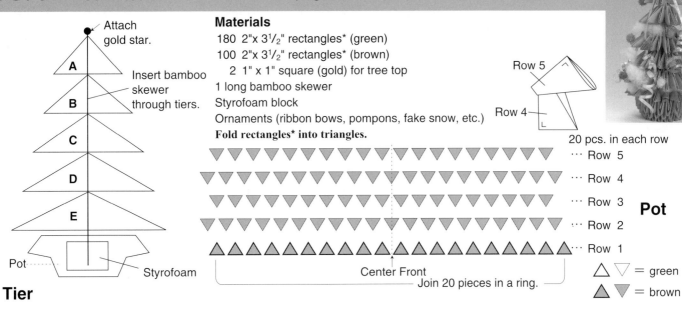

··· Row 5
··· Row 4
··· Row 3
··· Row 2
··· Row 1

Pot

Center Front
Join 20 pieces in a ring.

△ ▽ = green
▲ ▼ = brown

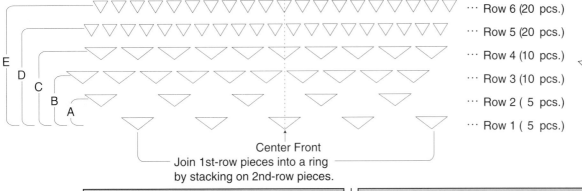

··· Row 6 (20 pcs.)
··· Row 5 (20 pcs.)
··· Row 4 (10 pcs.)
··· Row 3 (10 pcs.)
··· Row 2 (5 pcs.)
··· Row 1 (5 pcs.)

E
D
C
B
A

Center Front
Join 1st-row pieces into a ring
by stacking on 2nd-row pieces.

Actual Size Pattern

Tree top
(gold)

Make 2 and glue together.

❶ Tier A

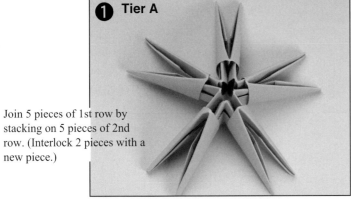

Join 5 pieces of 1st row by stacking on 5 pieces of 2nd row. (Interlock 2 pieces with a new piece.)

❸ Tier C

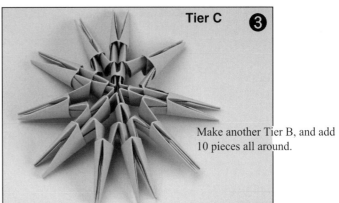

Make another Tier B, and add 10 pieces all around.

❷ Tier B

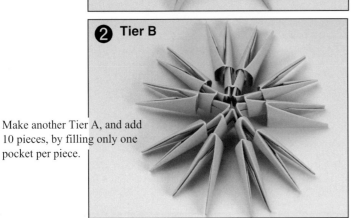

Make another Tier A, and add 10 pieces, by filling only one pocket per piece.

Tier E   Tier D

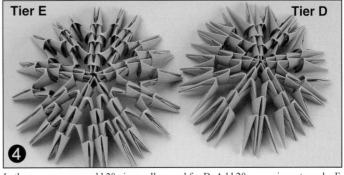

❹

In the same manner, add 20 pieces all around for D. Add 20 more pieces to make E.

22. Rooster (Satsuma) shown on page 22

Materials for Rooster with Pattern

439 $1^1/_2$" x $2^3/_4$" rectangles* (black/white pattern)
114 $1^1/_2$" x $2^3/_4$" rectangles* (white)
72 $1^1/_2$" x $2^3/_4$" rectangles* (gold)
1 $1^1/_2$" x $2^3/_4$" rectangle (yellow)
3 2" x 2" squares (red)

2 $^1/_8$" plastic joggle eyes
10 $3^1/_2$"L #20 wires
10 pcs. 4"L strings (gold/black)
2 pcs. 12"L strings (gold/black)
Fold rectangles* into triangles.

Crest

2" x 2"

(red)

Cut into triangles.

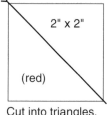

Insert
into head.

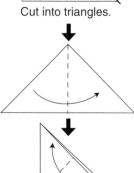

Body

Crest attaching position

△ ▽ = white
◬ ▽̇ = gold
△ ▽ = black/white pattern

Row 25 (5 pcs.)
Row 24 (6 pcs.)
Row 23 (6 pcs.)
Row 22 (7 pcs.)
Row 21 (9 pcs.)
Row 20 (9 pcs.)
Row 19 (11 pcs.)
Row 18 (11 pcs.)
Row 17 (11 pcs.)
Row 16 (11 pcs.)
Row 15 (11 pcs.)
Row 14 (11 pcs.)
Row 13 (11 pcs.)
Row 12 (11 pcs.)
Row 11 (12 pcs.)
Row 10 (13 pcs.)
Row 9 (14 pcs.)
Row 8 (15 pcs.)
Row 7 (22 pcs.)
Row 6 (22 pcs.)
Row 5 (22 pcs.)
Row 4 (22 pcs.)
Row 3 (22 pcs.)
Row 2 (22 pcs.)
Row 1 (22 pcs.)

Signs for piecing direction

▽ =

This side
faces out.

Double Pocket

△ =

This side
faces out.

Double Pocket

Join into a ring →
on this row.

Attach tail by gluing
onto 6 pcs. around
center.

Center Back

Insert
into chin.

Cut off.

Trim.

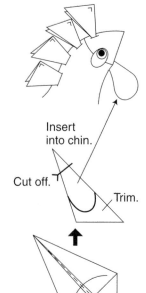

2" x 2"

(red)

Attach leg. Center Front

Join 1st-row pieces into a ring by stacking on 2nd-row pieces.

Tail

Curl and attach to back using glue gun.

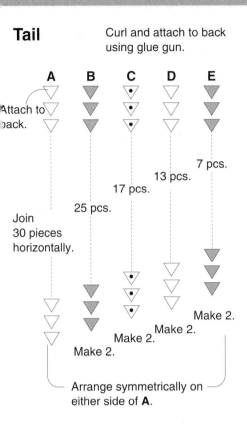

A	B	C	D	E

Attach to back.

Join 30 pieces horizontally.

7 pcs.

13 pcs.

17 pcs.

25 pcs.

Make 2.

Make 2.

Make 2.

Make 2.

Arrange symmetrically on either side of **A**.

Wings

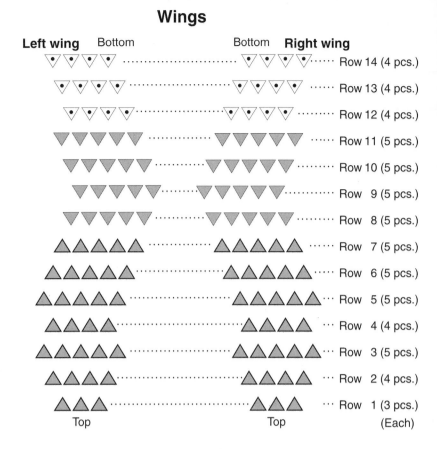

Left wing Bottom   Bottom **Right wing**

	Row 14 (4 pcs.)
	Row 13 (4 pcs.)
	Row 12 (4 pcs.)
	Row 11 (5 pcs.)
	Row 10 (5 pcs.)
	Row 9 (5 pcs.)
	Row 8 (5 pcs.)
	Row 7 (5 pcs.)
	Row 6 (5 pcs.)
	Row 5 (5 pcs.)
	Row 4 (4 pcs.)
	Row 3 (5 pcs.)
	Row 2 (4 pcs.)
	Row 1 (3 pcs.)

Top   Top   (Each)

Leg

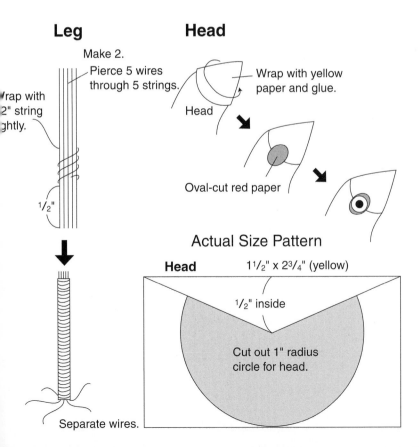

Make 2.
Pierce 5 wires through 5 strings.

Wrap with 2" string tightly.

$1/2$"

Separate wires.

Head

Wrap with yellow paper and glue.

Head

Oval-cut red paper

Actual Size Pattern

Head $1^1/2$" x $2^3/4$" (yellow)

$1/2$" inside

Cut out 1" radius circle for head.

Assembly

Use glue gun.

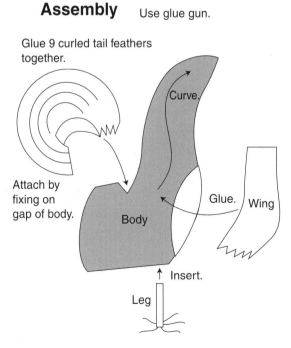

Glue 9 curled tail feathers together.

Attach by fixing on gap of body.

Curve.

Glue.

Wing

Body

Insert.

Leg

4.Mount Fuji shown on page 11

Materials

192 1 1/8" x 2 1/4" rectangles* (blue)

 79 1 1/8" x 2 1/4" rectangles* (white)

13 silk flowers

1 10" x 11" Shikishi (large square writing card)

Fold rectangles* into triangles.

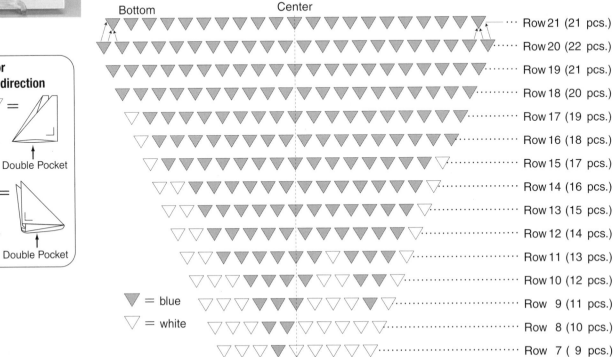

Bottom   Center

Row 21 (21 pcs.)
Row 20 (22 pcs.)
Row 19 (21 pcs.)
Row 18 (20 pcs.)
Row 17 (19 pcs.)
Row 16 (18 pcs.)
Row 15 (17 pcs.)
Row 14 (16 pcs.)
Row 13 (15 pcs.)
Row 12 (14 pcs.)
Row 11 (13 pcs.)
Row 10 (12 pcs.)
Row 9 (11 pcs.)
Row 8 (10 pcs.)
Row 7 (9 pcs.)
Row 6 (8 pcs.)
Row 5 (7 pcs.)
Row 4 (6 pcs.)
Row 3 (5 pcs.)
Row 2 (4 pcs.)
Row 1 (3 pcs.)

▼ = blue

▽ = white

Top

Signs for piecing direction

▽ =

This side faces out.

Double Pocket

△ =

This side faces out.

Double Pocket

Notes

• This project is made from a specially processed paper. See page 84 for information.

• Begin with top of the mountain, and glue pieces as you work.

• Lay the work flat as you stack on pieces.

• On every row, check that the pieces line up horizontally.

• When glue is dry, attach to the card and glue. Attach silk flower blossoms.

Treasure Boat

Note

Make the sides of the boat, and then add pieces to form bottom. When 5 side rows are done, interlock 2 extra rows with the bottom row, omitting 2 pcs. each at Center Front. Then shape Front by connecting separate parts with 2 pcs., then with 1 pc. as 2nd row. Reinforce the bottom with cardboard.

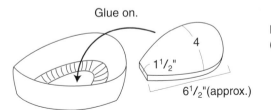

Glue on.

4

1 1/2"

6 1/2" (approx.)

Bottom asssembly

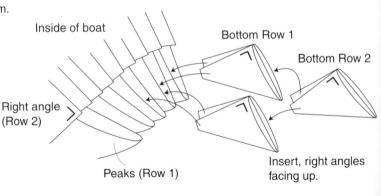

Inside of boat

Bottom Row 1

Bottom Row 2

Right angle (Row 2)

Peaks (Row 1)

Insert, right angles facing up.

6. Treasure Boat shown on page 12

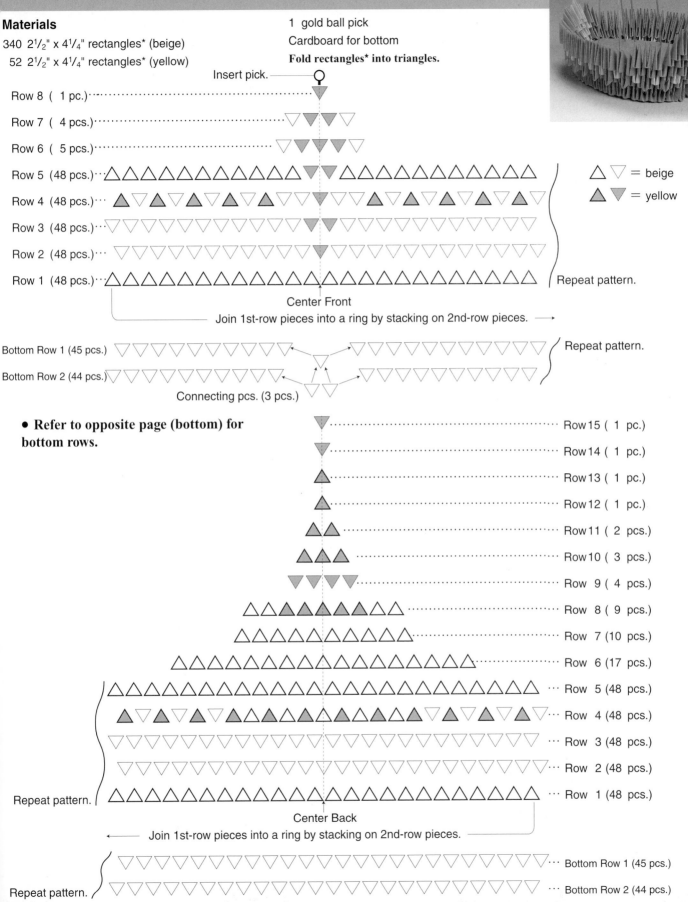

Materials

340 2½" x 4¼" rectangles* (beige)

52 2½" x 4¼" rectangles* (yellow)

1 gold ball pick

Cardboard for bottom

Fold rectangles* into triangles.

Insert pick.

Row 8 (1 pc.)

Row 7 (4 pcs.)

Row 6 (5 pcs.)

Row 5 (48 pcs.)

Row 4 (48 pcs.)

Row 3 (48 pcs.)

Row 2 (48 pcs.)

Row 1 (48 pcs.)

Center Front

△ ▽ = beige

▲ ▼ = yellow

Repeat pattern.

Join 1st-row pieces into a ring by stacking on 2nd-row pieces. →

Bottom Row 1 (45 pcs.)

Bottom Row 2 (44 pcs.)

Connecting pcs. (3 pcs.)

Repeat pattern.

• **Refer to opposite page (bottom) for bottom rows.**

Row 15 (1 pc.)

Row 14 (1 pc.)

Row 13 (1 pc.)

Row 12 (1 pc.)

Row 11 (2 pcs.)

Row 10 (3 pcs.)

Row 9 (4 pcs.)

Row 8 (9 pcs.)

Row 7 (10 pcs.)

Row 6 (17 pcs.)

Row 5 (48 pcs.)

Row 4 (48 pcs.)

Row 3 (48 pcs.)

Row 2 (48 pcs.)

Row 1 (48 pcs.)

Repeat pattern.

Center Back

Join 1st-row pieces into a ring by stacking on 2nd-row pieces.

Bottom Row 1 (45 pcs.)

Bottom Row 2 (44 pcs.)

Repeat pattern.

6.Kotobuki (Deity of long life) shown on page 12

▽ = white

▼ = black

△ ▽ = skin color

▲ ▼ = blue

△ = black/white stripes

Finished size: 1½"W x 4½"H

Materials

133 1⅛" x 2" rectangles* (blue)

52 1⅛" x 2" rectangles* (skin)

1 ½" square (skin) for hand

25 1⅛" x 2" rectangles* (black)

7 1⅛" x 2" rectangles* (stripes)

1 1⅛" x 2" rectangle* (white)

Felt (black for eyes, red for mouth)

Wool yarn (white for eyebrows and beard)

1 twig as walking stick

Fold rectangles* into triangles.

Right arm   **Left arm**

Insert and glue.

Pull out a flap and insert into body.   blue   skin color

Curl.

½" square (skin)

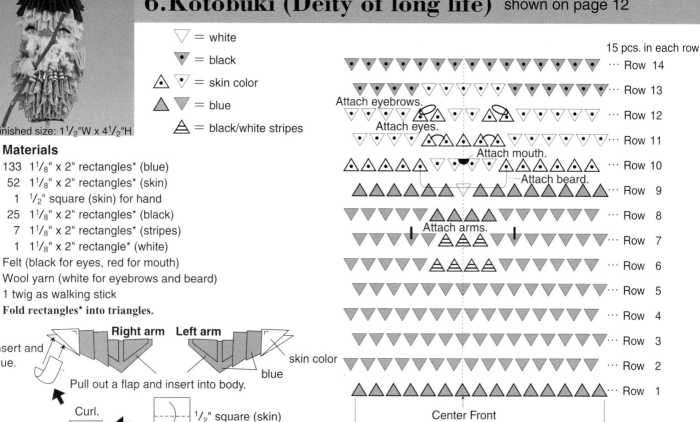

15 pcs. in each row

··· Row 14

··· Row 13

Attach eyebrows.   ··· Row 12

Attach eyes.   ··· Row 11

Attach mouth.   ··· Row 10

Attach beard.   ··· Row 9

Attach arms.   ··· Row 8

··· Row 7

··· Row 6

··· Row 5

··· Row 4

··· Row 3

··· Row 2

··· Row 1

Center Front
Join 15 pieces in a ring.

6.Bishamon (Deity of power) shown on page 12

△ ▽ = lavender/grey pattern

▲ ▼ = purple   △ = blue

△ ▽ = skin color   ▼ = black

● **Sword instructions on page 65**

Finished size: 2"W x 3¾"H

Materials

129 1⅛" x 2" rectangles* (pattern)

39 1⅛" x 2" rectangles* (skin)

2 ½" squares (skin) for hands

29 1⅛" x 2" rectangles* (purple)

27 1⅛" x 2" rectangles* (black)

9 1⅛" x 2" rectangles* (blue)

1 1½" x 2¾" rectangle (gold)

Felt (black for eyes and eyebrows, red for mouth)

1 wooden toothpick

Fold rectangles* into triangles.

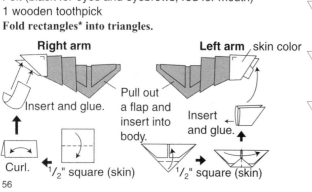

Right arm   **Left arm** skin color

Insert and glue.

Pull out a flap and insert into body.

Insert and glue.

Curl.   ½" square (skin)   ½" square (skin)

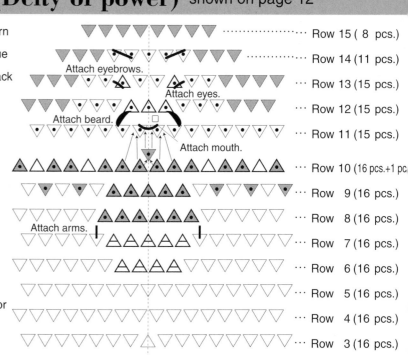

·················· Row 15 (8 pcs.)

Attach eyebrows.   ············ Row 14 (11 pcs.)

Attach eyes.   ··· Row 13 (15 pcs.)

Attach beard.   ··· Row 12 (15 pcs.)

Attach mouth.   ··· Row 11 (15 pcs.)

··· Row 10 (16 pcs.+1 pc)

··· Row 9 (16 pcs.)

··· Row 8 (16 pcs.)

Attach arms.   ··· Row 7 (16 pcs.)

··· Row 6 (16 pcs.)

··· Row 5 (16 pcs.)

··· Row 4 (16 pcs.)

··· Row 3 (16 pcs.)

··· Row 2 (16 pcs.)

··· Row 1 (16 pcs.)

Center Front
Join 15 pieces in a ring.

6.Hotei (Deity of abundance)　shown on page 12

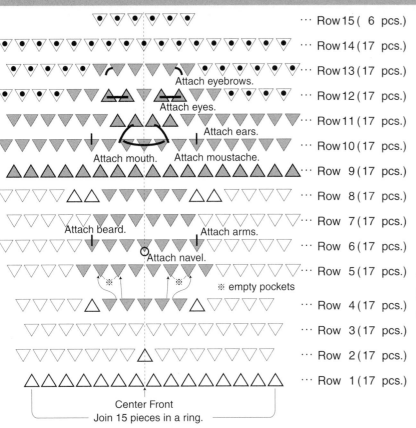

··· Row 15 (6 pcs.)
··· Row 14 (17 pcs.)
··· Row 13 (17 pcs.) Attach eyebrows.
··· Row 12 (17 pcs.) Attach eyes.
··· Row 11 (17 pcs.) Attach ears.
··· Row 10 (17 pcs.) Attach mouth. Attach moustache.
··· Row 9 (17 pcs.)
··· Row 8 (17 pcs.)
··· Row 7 (17 pcs.) Attach beard. Attach arms.
··· Row 6 (17 pcs.) Attach navel.
··· Row 5 (17 pcs.) ※ empty pockets
··· Row 4 (17 pcs.)
··· Row 3 (17 pcs.)
··· Row 2 (17 pcs.)
··· Row 1 (17 pcs.)

Center Front
Join 15 pieces in a ring.

Finished size:
$2\frac{1}{4}$"W x $9\frac{1}{2}$"H

●Pattern of fan on page 65.

△(grey) ▽ = skin color
△ ▽ = light green
△(dot) ▼(dot) = black

Materials
- 101　$1\frac{1}{2}$" x 2" rectangles* (skin)
- 1　$\frac{1}{2}$" square (skin) for hand
- 101　$1\frac{1}{8}$" x 2" rectangles* (light green)
- 42　$1\frac{1}{8}$" x 2" rectangles* (black)
- 2　$1\frac{1}{2}$" square (dark brown)
- Felt (black for eyes, eyebrows and moustache, red for mouth, white for navel)
- 1 wooden toothpick

Fold rectangles* into triangles.

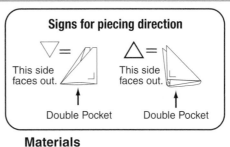

$\frac{1}{2}$" square (skin)　Curl.
Insert and glue.
Right arm　light green　**Left arm**
Pull out a flap and insert into body.　skin color
Ear　Insert.

6.Fukurokuju (Deity of happiness)　shown on page 12

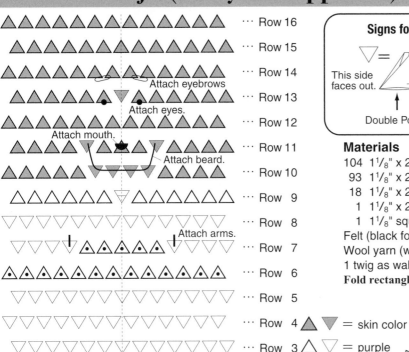

··· Row 16
··· Row 15
··· Row 14 Attach eyebrows
··· Row 13 Attach eyes.
··· Row 12
··· Row 11 Attach mouth.
··· Row 10 Attach beard.
··· Row 9
··· Row 8
··· Row 7 Attach arms.
··· Row 6
··· Row 5
··· Row 4
··· Row 3
··· Row 2
··· Row 1
13 pcs. in each row

Center Front
Join 13 pieces in a ring.

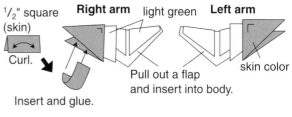

Signs for piecing direction

▽ = This side faces out. Double Pocket
△ = This side faces out. Double Pocket

Finished size: $1\frac{3}{4}$"W x 3"H

Materials
- 104　$1\frac{1}{8}$" x 2" rectangles* (purple pattern)
- 93　$1\frac{1}{8}$" x 2" rectangles* (skin)
- 18　$1\frac{1}{8}$" x 2" rectangles* (grey)
- 1　$1\frac{1}{8}$" x 2" rectangle* (blue)
- 1　$1\frac{1}{8}$" square (skin) for hand
- Felt (black for eyes, red for mouth, white for navel)
- Wool yarn (white for eyebrows and beard)
- 1 twig as walking stick

Fold rectangles* into triangles.

△(grey) ▼ = skin color
△ ▽ = purple pattern
△(dot) = grey
▽ = blue

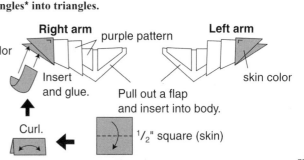

Right arm　purple pattern　**Left arm**
Insert and glue.
Pull out a flap and insert into body.　skin color
Curl.　$\frac{1}{2}$" square (skin)

Finished size:
2"W x 3³/₄"H

6. Benzai (Goddess of arts) shown on page 12

△ ▽ = red
▼ = black
△ = skin color
▽• = pink
▼• = purple

Materials

108 1¹/₈" x 2" rectangles*(red)
64 1¹/₈" x 2" rectangles*(black)
20 1¹/₈" x 2" rectangles*(skin)
16 1¹/₈" x 2" rectangles*(pink)
3 1¹/₈" x 2" rectangles*(purple)
Felt (black for eyes, red for mouth)
Biwa: Cardboard, brown Washi paper, wire
Fold rectangles* into triangles.

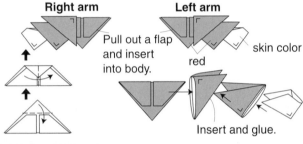

Right arm

Left arm

Pull out a flap and insert into body.

red

skin color

Insert and glue.

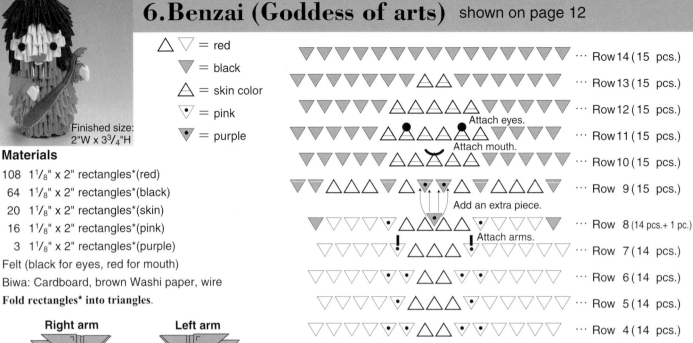

··· Row 14 (15 pcs.)
··· Row 13 (15 pcs.)
··· Row 12 (15 pcs.)
Attach eyes.
··· Row 11 (15 pcs.)
Attach mouth.
··· Row 10 (15 pcs.)
··· Row 9 (15 pcs.)
Add an extra piece.
··· Row 8 (14 pcs.+ 1 pc.)
Attach arms.
··· Row 7 (14 pcs.)
··· Row 6 (14 pcs.)
··· Row 5 (14 pcs.)
··· Row 4 (14 pcs.)
··· Row 3 (14 pcs.)
··· Row 2 (14 pcs.)
··· Row 1 (14 pcs.)

Center Front
Join 14 pieces in a ring.

● **Pattern of Biwa,
a musical instrument,
on page 65.**

---

6. Ebisu (Deity of integrity) shown on page 12

▼• = red
△ ▽ = skin color
△ = beige
△• ▽• = blue/white pattern
△ ▼ = blue

Materials

101 1¹/₈" x 2" rectangles*(blue)
53 1¹/₈" x 2" rectangles*(red)
45 1¹/₈" x 2" rectangles*(skin)
1 ¹/₂" square (skin) for hand
34 1¹/₈" x 2" rectangles* (pattern)
1 1¹/₈" x 2" rectangle* (beige)
17 1¹/₈" x 2" rectangles* (red) for fish
Felt (black for eyebrows, eyes and beard, red for mouth)
¹/₈"L bamboo shape stick for fishing rod
¹/₈"W x 8"L gold ribbon   Narrow elastic (gold)
Fold rectangles* into triangles.

Finished size:
2¹/₄"W x 3¹/₂"H

Right arm Pull out a flap and insert into body. **Left arm**

skin color
blue
color

Insert and glue.

Curl.

¹/₂" square (skin)

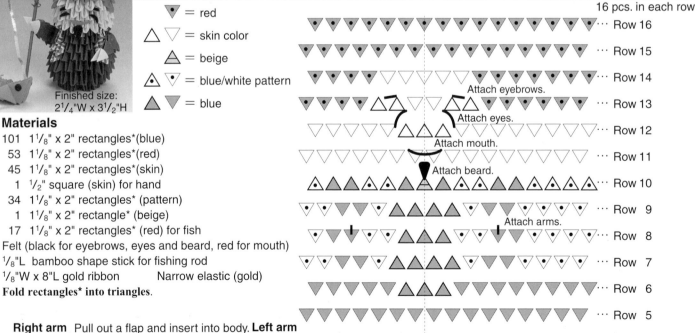

16 pcs. in each row
··· Row 16
··· Row 15
··· Row 14
Attach eyebrows.
··· Row 13
Attach eyes.
··· Row 12
Attach mouth.
··· Row 11
Attach beard.
··· Row 10
··· Row 9
Attach arms.
··· Row 8
··· Row 7
··· Row 6
··· Row 5
··· Row 4
··· Row 3

Center Front
Join 16 pieces in a ring.

● **Pattern of fish
on page 65.**

6. Daikoku (Deity of wealth) shown on page 12

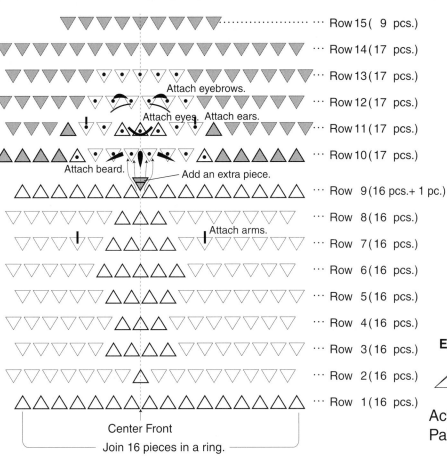

··· Row 15 (9 pcs.)
··· Row 14 (17 pcs.)
··· Row 13 (17 pcs.)
Attach eyebrows.
··· Row 12 (17 pcs.)
Attach eyes. Attach ears.
··· Row 11 (17 pcs.)
··· Row 10 (17 pcs.)
Attach beard. Add an extra piece.
··· Row 9 (16 pcs.+ 1 pc.)
··· Row 8 (16 pcs.)
Attach arms.
··· Row 7 (16 pcs.)
··· Row 6 (16 pcs.)
··· Row 5 (16 pcs.)
··· Row 4 (16 pcs.)
··· Row 3 (16 pcs.)
··· Row 2 (16 pcs.)
··· Row 1 (16 pcs.)

Center Front
Join 16 pieces in a ring.

△ ▽ = blue
△ ▼ = green
⊡ ⊡ = skin
▽ = purple

Finished size: 2"W x 3 3/4"H

Materials

150 1 1/8" x 2" rectangles*(blue)
 68 1 1/8" x 2" rectangles*(green)
 30 1 1/8" x 2" rectangles*(skin)
  1 1/2" square (skin) for hand
  1 1 1/8" x 2" rectangle*(purple)
Washi paper (dark brown, beige) for mallet
Felt (black for eyebrows,
    eyes and beard, red for mouth)
6" square unwoven fabric (white) for bag
1/8"W x 6"L gold ribbon
1 wooden toothpick
Fold rectangles* into triangles.

Ear   Make 2.   Insert.

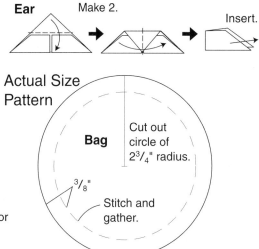

Actual Size Pattern

Cut out circle of 2 3/4" radius.

Bag

3/8"

Stitch and gather.

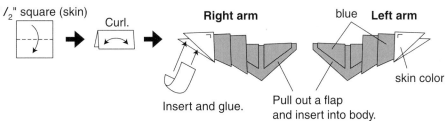

/2" square (skin)   Curl.   **Right arm**   blue **Left arm**

skin color

Insert and glue.   Pull out a flap and insert into body.

Mallet   1/2" diameter

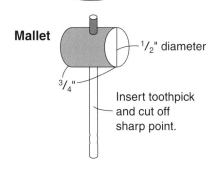

3/4"

Insert toothpick and cut off sharp point.

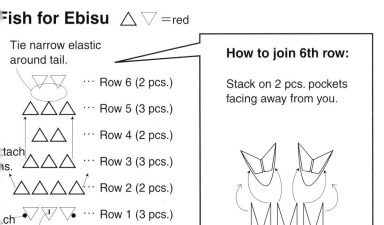

Fish for Ebisu △ ▽ = red

Tie narrow elastic around tail.

··· Row 6 (2 pcs.)
··· Row 5 (3 pcs.)
··· Row 4 (2 pcs.)
··· Row 3 (3 pcs.)
··· Row 2 (2 pcs.)
··· Row 1 (3 pcs.)
Insert ribbon.

How to join 6th row:

Stack on 2 pcs. pockets facing away from you.

Signs for piecing direction

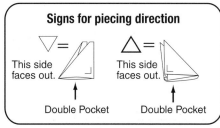

▽ = This side faces out.   △ = This side faces out.

Double Pocket   Double Pocket

Materials

124 1⅛" x 2" rectangles* (blue)
119 1⅛" x 2" rectangles* (pattern)
4 1⅛" x 2" rectangles* (skin)
11 1⅛" x 2" rectangles* (white)
1 1⅛" x 2" rectangle* (pink)
Sleeves: 2 2½" x 4¼" rectangles (pattern)
4 ⅜" x 2" rectangles (pink)
2 ⅜" x 2" rectangles (yellow)

Head : 1¾" W wooden ball
1 bamboo skewer
Hair : Wool yarn (grey)
Cotton thread (neutral)
Broom : 1⅛" x 2¾" Washi (ocher)
1 thick bamboo skewer w/ handle

Fold rectangles* into triangles.

△ ▽ = white
▲ ▼ = pattern
△ ▽ = blue
▼• = pink

Broom

Bamboo skewer
with wide handle

Wrap with Washi
and glue.

Actual Size Pattern

Body

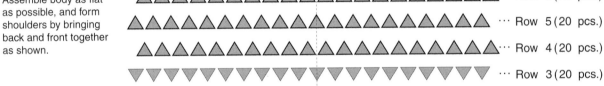

Fill gap with an extra piece.

Row 14 (12 pcs.+ 1 pc.)
Row 13 (14 pcs.)
Row 12 (14 pcs.)
Row 11 (16 pcs.)
Row 10 (18 pcs.)
Row 9 (20 pcs.)
Row 8 (20 pcs.)
Row 7 (20 pcs.)
Row 6 (20 pcs.)
Row 5 (20 pcs.)
Row 4 (20 pcs.)
Row 3 (20 pcs.)
Row 2 (20 pcs.)
Row 1 (20 pcs.)

Center Front
Join 20 pieces in a ring.

Back
Push Front

Assemble body as flat
as possible, and form
shoulders by bringing
back and front together
as shown.

Sleeve Make 2.

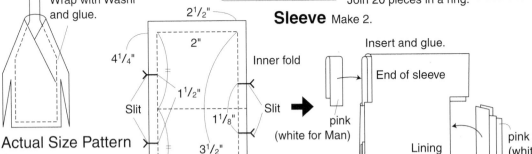

2½"
2"
4¼"
1½"
3½"
1⅛"
Slit
Inner fold
Slit

Insert and glue.

End of sleeve

pink
(white for Man)

Lining

pink
(white for Man)

yellow
(blue for Man)

Hand Make 2.

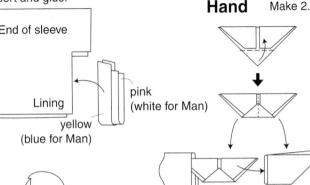

Use 1 pc.
open.

Fold 1 pc.

Sleeve

Head

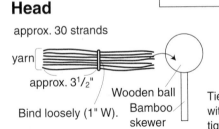

approx. 30 strands
yarn
approx. 3½"
Bind loosely (1" W).

Wooden ball
Bamboo
skewer

Tie hair and neck
with cotton thread
tightly.

Tie with gold
elastic.

7. Golden Age Couple (Woman) shown on page 13

Materials

163 1⅛" x 2" rectangles* (pattern)
130 1⅛" x 2" rectangles* (grey)
15 1⅛" x 2" rectangles* (white)
5 1⅛" x 2" rectangles* (skin)
Sleeves: 2 2½" x 4¼" rectangles (pattern)
4 ⅜" x 2" rectangles (white)
2 ⅜" x 2" rectangles (blue)

Hood : 1 2" x 3½" rectangle (grey)
Headband : 1 ¼" x 3½" rectangle (pattern)
Head : 1 1" W wooden ball
1 bamboo skewer
Hair : Fine knitting yarn (beige)
Broom : 1 2" x 4" Washi (ocher)
1 thick bamboo skewer w/ handle
1 wooden toothpick

Fold rectangles* into triangles.

Legend

▼ = skin color
▲ ▼ = grey
△ ▽ = pattern
△ ▽ = white

Broom

Bamboo skewer with wide handle

Actual Size Pattern

Wrap with Washi and glue.

Glue on toothpick.

Body

Fill gap with an extra piece.

··· Row 17 (16 pcs.+ 1 pc.)
··· Row 16 (14 pcs.)
··· Row 15 (16 pcs.)
··· Row 14 (16 pcs.)
··· Row 13 (16 pcs.)
··· Row 12 (16 pcs.)
··· Row 11 (18 pcs.)
··· Row 10 (16 pcs.)
··· Row 9 (18 pcs.)
··· Row 8 (20 pcs.)
··· Row 7 (18 pcs.)
··· Row 6 (20 pcs.)
··· Row 5 (20 pcs.)
··· Row 4 (20 pcs.)
··· Row 3 (20 pcs.)

Foot attaching position — Foot attaching position
··· Row 2 (20 pcs.)
··· Row 1 (20 pcs.)

Center Front — Center Back

Join 20 pieces in a ring

Signs for piecing direction

▽ = This side faces out. Double Pocket

△ = This side faces out. Double Pocket

Head

approx. 10 strands yarn — grey

Wooden ball — Bamboo skewer

2" ¼" 1/16"

Fold. Fold backwards.

Bind yarn and tie around neck.

Foot
Make 2.

white

Insert into body.

● **Make sleeves and hands referring to opposite page.**

8. Mouse shown on page 14

Materials

390 2" x 3½" rectangles*(grey)
  2 2¾" x 5" rectangles (grey) for ears and limbs
  1 2" x 3½" rectangle (pink) for ears
2 ½" plastic joggle eyes
⅓" x ⅜" oval felt (black) for muzzle
3 2¾"L #22 wires (black) for whiskers
8" pipe cleaners (silver) for tail

Fold rectangles* into triangles.

△ ▽ =grey

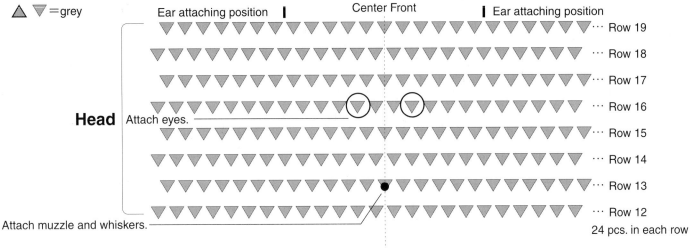

Head

Attach eyes.

Attach muzzle and whiskers.

Ear attaching position | Center Front | Ear attaching position

··· Row 19
··· Row 18
··· Row 17
··· Row 16
··· Row 15
··· Row 14
··· Row 13
··· Row 12

24 pcs. in each row

Actual Size Patterns

Ear

Fold

Hand

Body

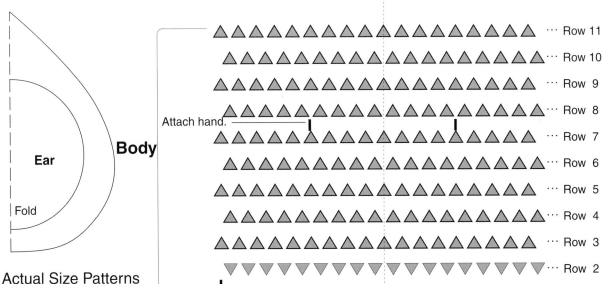

Attach hand.

Attach tail.

··· Row 11
··· Row 10
··· Row 9
··· Row 8
··· Row 7
··· Row 6
··· Row 5
··· Row 4
··· Row 3
··· Row 2
··· Row 1

Center Front

18 pcs. in each row

Join 18 pieces in a ring.

Increasing on Row 12

Center Front

Row 12 (18 pcs.+ 6 pcs.)

Row 11 (18 pcs.)

+ 1 pc.   + 1 pc.   + 1 pc.   + 1 pc.   + 1 pc.   + 1 pc.

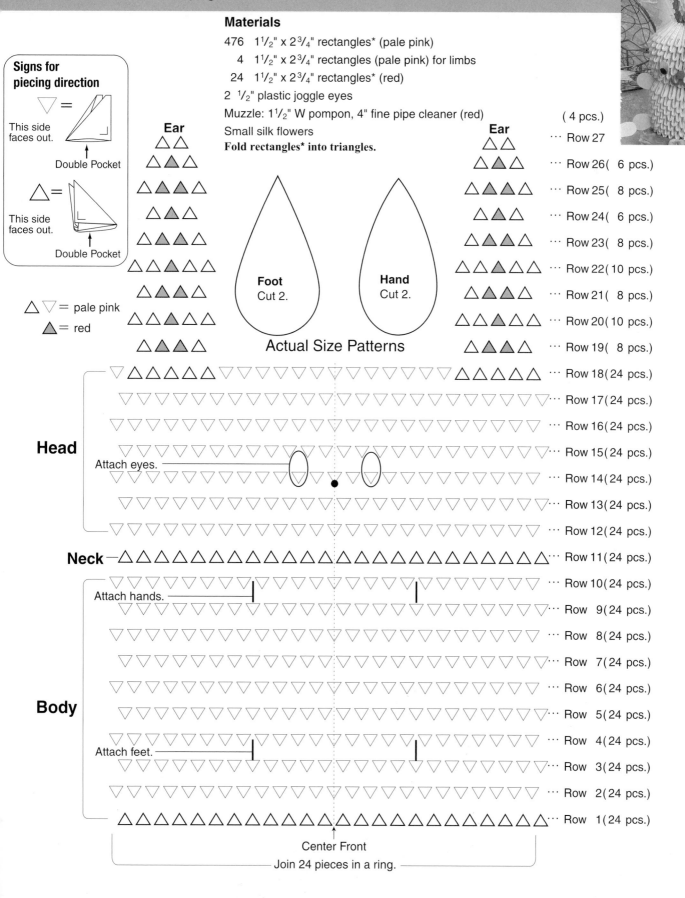

Signs for piecing direction

▽ =

This side faces out.

Double Pocket

△ =

This side faces out.

Double Pocket

△ ▽ = pale pink

△ = red

Materials

476 1½" x 2¾" rectangles* (pale pink)

4 1½" x 2¾" rectangles (pale pink) for limbs

24 1½" x 2¾" rectangles* (red)

2 ½" plastic joggle eyes

Muzzle: 1½" W pompon, 4" fine pipe cleaner (red) (4 pcs.)

Small silk flowers

Fold rectangles* into triangles.

Ear

Foot
Cut 2.

Hand
Cut 2.

Actual Size Patterns

Ear

··· Row 27

··· Row 26(6 pcs.)

··· Row 25(8 pcs.)

··· Row 24(6 pcs.)

··· Row 23(8 pcs.)

··· Row 22(10 pcs.)

··· Row 21(8 pcs.)

··· Row 20(10 pcs.)

··· Row 19(8 pcs.)

··· Row 18(24 pcs.)

··· Row 17(24 pcs.)

··· Row 16(24 pcs.)

··· Row 15(24 pcs.)

Head

Attach eyes.

··· Row 14(24 pcs.)

··· Row 13(24 pcs.)

··· Row 12(24 pcs.)

Neck ··· Row 11(24 pcs.)

Attach hands.

··· Row 10(24 pcs.)

··· Row 9(24 pcs.)

··· Row 8(24 pcs.)

··· Row 7(24 pcs.)

··· Row 6(24 pcs.)

Body

··· Row 5(24 pcs.)

··· Row 4(24 pcs.)

Attach feet.

··· Row 3(24 pcs.)

··· Row 2(24 pcs.)

··· Row 1(24 pcs.)

Center Front

Join 24 pieces in a ring.

63

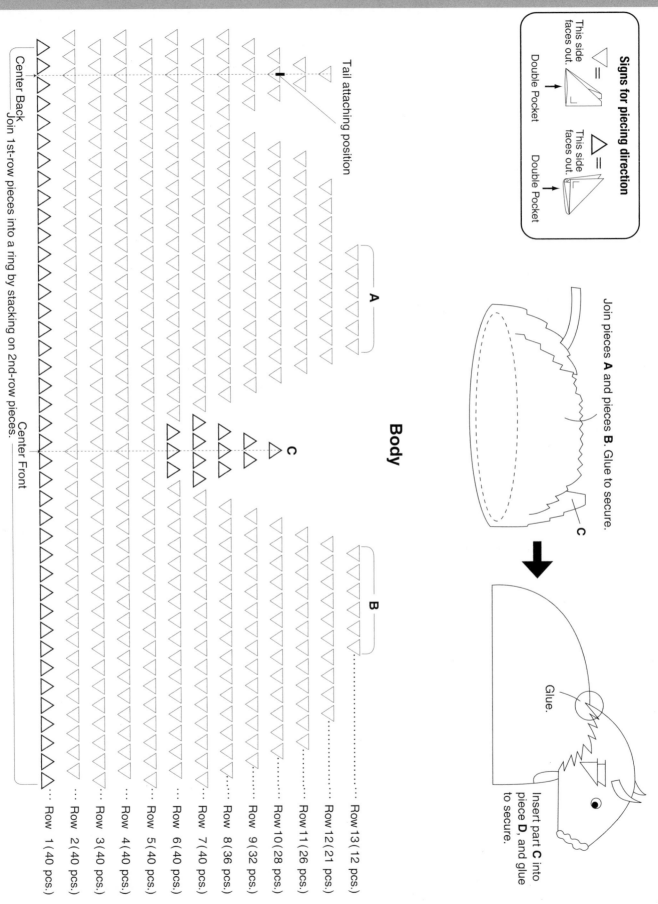

Signs for piecing direction

⊿ = This side faces out.

Double Pocket

△ = This side faces out.

Double Pocket

Join pieces **A** and pieces **B**. Glue to secure.

C

Glue.

Insert part **C** into piece **D**, and glue to secure.

Body

Tail attaching position

A

C

B

Center Back. Join 1st-row pieces into a ring by stacking on 2nd-row pieces.

Center Front

Row 13 (12 pcs.)
Row 12 (21 pcs.)
Row 11 (26 pcs.)
Row 10 (28 pcs.)
Row 9 (32 pcs.)
Row 8 (36 pcs.)
Row 7 (40 pcs.)
Row 6 (40 pcs.)
Row 5 (40 pcs.)
Row 4 (40 pcs.)
Row 3 (40 pcs.)
Row 2 (40 pcs.)
Row 1 (40 pcs.)

Materials for Brown Ox

585   $1\frac{1}{2}$" x $2\frac{3}{4}$" rectangles* (dark brown)

10   $\frac{3}{4}$" x $1\frac{1}{2}$" rectangles* (dark brown)

12   $1\frac{1}{2}$" x $2\frac{3}{4}$" rectangles* (light brown)

3   $\frac{1}{2}$" x 8" Yuzen Washi paper for saddlecloth

Approx. 1 yd. cording with fringes (red)

2   $\frac{3}{8}$" plastic joggle eyes

1   wooden toothpick

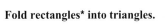

Fold rectangles* into triangles.

Head

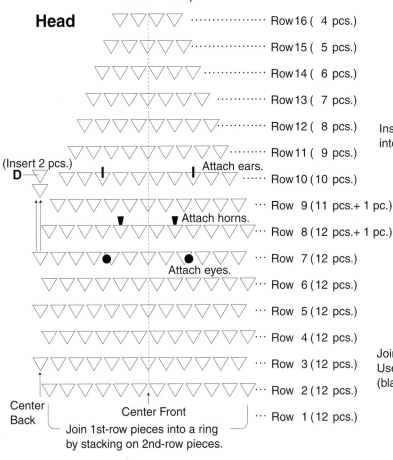

Row 16 (4 pcs.)
Row 15 (5 pcs.)
Row 14 (6 pcs.)
Row 13 (7 pcs.)
Row 12 (8 pcs.)
Row 11 (9 pcs.)
(Insert 2 pcs.)
D — Attach ears. Row 10 (10 pcs.)
Row 9 (11 pcs.+ 1 pc.)
Attach horns. Row 8 (12 pcs.+ 1 pc.)
Attach eyes. Row 7 (12 pcs.)
Row 6 (12 pcs.)
Row 5 (12 pcs.)
Row 4 (12 pcs.)
Row 3 (12 pcs.)
Row 2 (12 pcs.)
Center Back   Center Front   Row 1 (12 pcs.)

Join 1st-row pieces into a ring by stacking on 2nd-row pieces.

Tail

Insert into body.

Join 10 pieces horizontally.
Use dark brown for Brown Ox.
(black for Holstein)

Horn

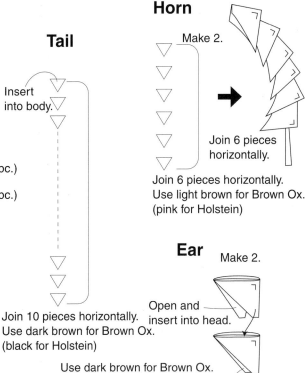

Make 2.

Join 6 pieces horizontally.

Join 6 pieces horizontally.
Use light brown for Brown Ox.
(pink for Holstein)

Ear

Make 2.

Open and insert into head.

Use dark brown for Brown Ox.
(black for Holstein)

Glue.

● Holstein materials and patterns on page 89.

Bishamon Sword

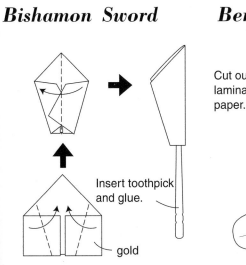

Insert toothpick and glue.

gold

Benzaiten Biwa (lute)

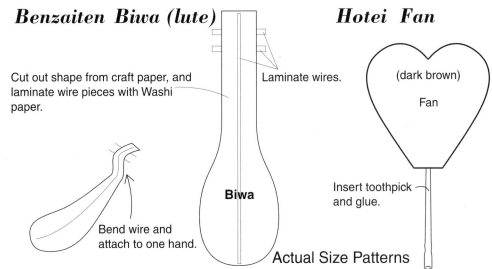

Cut out shape from craft paper, and laminate wire pieces with Washi paper.

Laminate wires.

Bend wire and attach to one hand.

Biwa

Hotei Fan

(dark brown)

Fan

Insert toothpick and glue.

Actual Size Patterns

Materials

201 2"x 3½" rectangles* (gold)
 31 1½" x 2¾" rectangles* (silver)
6   5"L Mizuhiki cording (gold)
1   10" pipe cleaner (silver)
2   6mm round beads (black) for eyes
1   1½" Styrofoam ball
#28 wire
Kitchen foil

Fold rectangles* into triangles.

Head

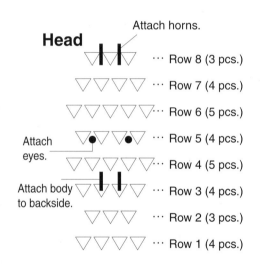

Attach horns.
··· Row 8 (3 pcs.)
··· Row 7 (4 pcs.)
··· Row 6 (5 pcs.)
Attach eyes. ··· Row 5 (4 pcs.)
··· Row 4 (5 pcs.)
Attach body to backside. ··· Row 3 (4 pcs.)
··· Row 2 (3 pcs.)
··· Row 1 (4 pcs.)

Body

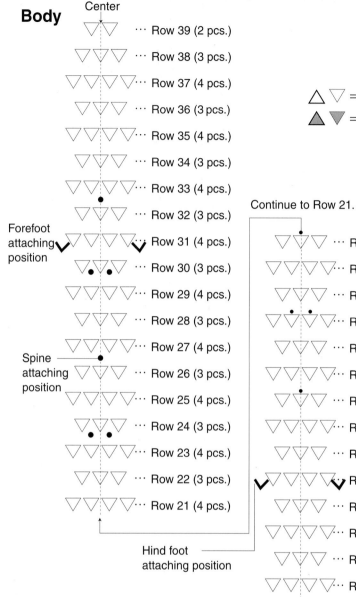

Center
··· Row 39 (2 pcs.)
··· Row 38 (3 pcs.)
··· Row 37 (4 pcs.)
··· Row 36 (3 pcs.)
··· Row 35 (4 pcs.)
··· Row 34 (3 pcs.)
··· Row 33 (4 pcs.)
··· Row 32 (3 pcs.)
Forefoot attaching position ··· Row 31 (4 pcs.)
··· Row 30 (3 pcs.)
··· Row 29 (4 pcs.)
··· Row 28 (3 pcs.)
··· Row 27 (4 pcs.)
Spine attaching position ··· Row 26 (3 pcs.)
··· Row 25 (4 pcs.)
··· Row 24 (3 pcs.)
··· Row 23 (4 pcs.)
··· Row 22 (3 pcs.)
··· Row 21 (4 pcs.)

△ ▽ = gold
▲ ▼ = silver

Continue to Row 21.

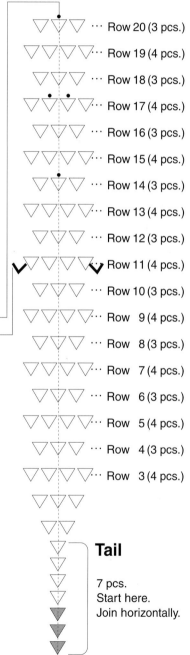

··· Row 20 (3 pcs.)
··· Row 19 (4 pcs.)
··· Row 18 (3 pcs.)
··· Row 17 (4 pcs.)
··· Row 16 (3 pcs.)
··· Row 15 (4 pcs.)
··· Row 14 (3 pcs.)
··· Row 13 (4 pcs.)
··· Row 12 (3 pcs.)
··· Row 11 (4 pcs.)
··· Row 10 (3 pcs.)
··· Row 9 (4 pcs.)
··· Row 8 (3 pcs.)
··· Row 7 (4 pcs.)
··· Row 6 (3 pcs.)
··· Row 5 (4 pcs.)
··· Row 4 (3 pcs.)
··· Row 3 (4 pcs.)

Hind foot attaching position

Tail

7 pcs.
Start here.
Join horizontally.

Signs for piecing direction

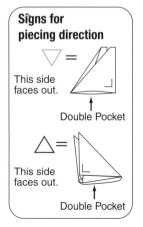

▽ = This side faces out. Double Pocket

△ = This side faces out. Double Pocket

Horn   ## Forefoot   ## Hind foot

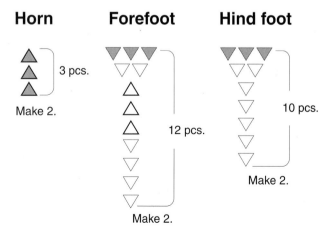

3 pcs.
Make 2.

12 pcs.
Make 2.

10 pcs.
Make 2.

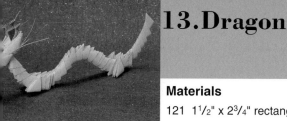

13. Dragon
14. Snake

shown on page 17

Dragon

Snake

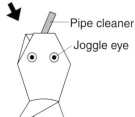

Materials

121 1½" x 2¾" rectangles*
      (lime green)
  2   1½" x 2¾" rectangles* (gold)
  6   3"L Mizuhiki cording
  2   6mm round beads (black) for eyes
#28 wire

Fold rectangles* into triangles.

Materials per Snake

57 2"x 3½" rectangles* (light brown)
 1 2"x 3½" rectangle
     (light brown) for head
 2 14"L #22 wires
 2 ¼" plastic joggle eyes
 2" fine pipe cleaners (red)

Fold rectangles* into triangles.

Body

Center

▽▽ ··· Row 45 (2 pcs.)
▽ ··· Row 44 (1 pc.)
▽▽ ··· Row 43 (2 pcs.)
▽ ··· Row 42 (1 pc.)
▽▽ ··· Row 41 (2 pcs.)
▽ ··· Row 40 (1 pc.)
▽▽ ··· Row 39 (2 pcs.)
▽ ··· Row 38 (1 pc.)
▽▽ ··· Row 37 (2 pcs.)
▽ ··· Row 36 (1 pc.)
▽▽ ··· Row 35 (2 pcs.)
▽ ··· Row 34 (1 pc.)
▽▽ ··· Row 33 (2 pcs.)
Attach forefeet.
▽ ··· Row 32 (1 pc.)
▽▽ ··· Row 31 (2 pcs.)
▽ ··· Row 30 (1 pc.)
▽▽ ··· Row 29 (2 pcs.)
▽ ··· Row 28 (1 pc.)
▽▽ ··· Row 27 (2 pcs.)
▽ ··· Row 26 (1 pc.)
▽▽ ··· Row 25 (2 pcs.)
▽ ··· Row 24 (1 pc.)
▽▽ ··· Row 23 (2 pcs.)
▽ ··· Row 22 (1 pc.)
▽▽ ··· Row 21 (2 pcs.)

Continue to Row 21.

▽ ··· Row 20 (1 pc.)
▽▽ ··· Row 19 (2 pcs.)
▽ ··· Row 18 (1 pc.)
▽▽ ··· Row 17 (2 pcs.)
▽ ··· Row 16 (1 pc.)
▽▽ ··· Row 15 (2 pcs.)
▽ ··· Row 14 (1 pc.)
▽▽ ··· Row 13 (2 pcs.)
▽ ··· Row 12 (1 pc.)
▽▽ ··· Row 11 (2 pcs.)
▽ ··· Row 10 (1 pc.)
▽▽ ··· Row 9 (2 pcs.)
▽ ··· Row 8 (1 pc.)
▽▽ ··· Row 7 (2 pcs.)
▽ ··· Row 6 (1 pc.)
▽▽ ··· Row 5 (2 pcs.)
▽ ··· Row 4 (1 pc.)
▽▽ ··· Row 3 (2 pcs.)
▽ ··· Row 2 (1 pc.)
▽▽ ··· Row 1 (2 pcs.)
Attach hind feet.

Tail
7 pcs.

Start here.

▽ =lime green

Snake Body

Attach head.

△
△
▽
△
Body

Join 50 pieces horizontally.

▽
△
▽
△
▽
▽
▽
▽
Tail
7 pcs.
▽
▽
▽
▽

Inserting 2 wires, assemble by alternating piece direction.

Wire

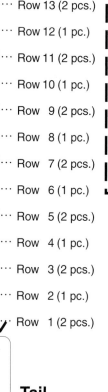

Head

3½"

2"

3/8"

Fold in and unfold. Push corners inside.

Fold in and glue.

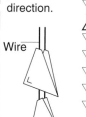

Pipe cleaner
Joggle eye

Head

Attach horns (gold)

▮▽▽▽▮ ··· Row 8 (3 pcs.)
▽▽▽▽ ··· Row 7 (4 pcs.)
●▽▽▽● ··· Row 6 (3 pcs.)
Attach eyes.
▽▽ ··· Row 5 (2 pcs.)
▽×▽×▽ ··· Row 4 (3 pcs.)
Attach body.
▽▽ ··· Row 3 (2 pcs.)
▽▽▽ ··· Row 2 (3 pcs.)
▽▽ ··· Row 1 (2 pcs.)

Foot

▽▽
▽
▽
▽
6 pcs.

Make 4.

19.Monkey (Pair) shown on page 20

Materials per Monkey

- 371 $1\frac{1}{2}$" x $2\frac{3}{4}$" rectangles*(light brown)
- 66 $1\frac{1}{2}$" x $2\frac{3}{4}$" rectangles*(red)
- 120 $1\frac{1}{2}$" x $2\frac{3}{4}$" rectangles*(green/orange) for vest
- 24 $1\frac{1}{2}$" x $2\frac{3}{4}$" rectangles* (dark brown)
- 1 $1\frac{1}{2}$" square (red) for head

Felt (dark brown) for ears

2 pcs. $2\frac{1}{4}$" string (red)

Fold rectangles* into triangles.

Actual Size Pattern

Face

1.Begin with bottom and work toward back.

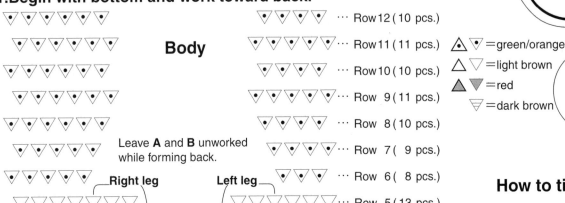

Body

Leave **A** and **B** unworked while forming back.

Row 12 (10 pcs.)
Row 11 (11 pcs.)
Row 10 (10 pcs.)
Row 9 (11 pcs.)
Row 8 (10 pcs.)
Row 7 (9 pcs.)
Row 6 (8 pcs.)
Row 5 (13 pcs.)
Row 4 (14 pcs.)
Row 3 (18 pcs.)
Row 2 (18 pcs.)
Row 1 (18 pcs.)

Right leg **Left leg**

Belly

Attach tail.

Center Front
Join 18 pieces in a ring.

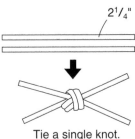

=green/orange
=light brown
=red
=dark brown

Ear
Cut 2.

How to tie string

$2\frac{1}{4}$"

Tie a single knot.

2.Make front body.

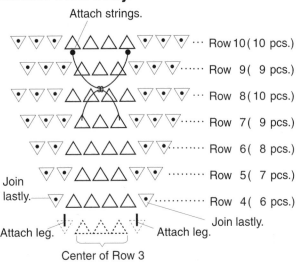

Attach strings.

Row 10(10 pcs.)
Row 9 (9 pcs.)
Row 8 (10 pcs.)
Row 7 (9 pcs.)
Row 6 (8 pcs.)
Row 5 (7 pcs.)
Row 4 (6 pcs.)

Join lastly.

Attach leg.   Attach leg.

Join lastly.

Center of Row 3

3.Make legs.

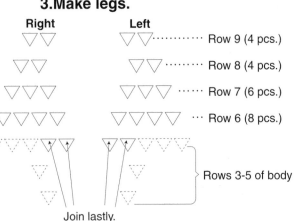

Right **Left**

Row 9 (4 pcs.)
Row 8 (4 pcs.)
Row 7 (6 pcs.)
Row 6 (8 pcs.)

Join lastly.

Rows 3-5 of body

Signs for piecing direction

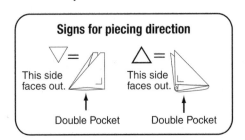

= This side faces out.

= This side faces out.

Double Pocket   Double Pocket

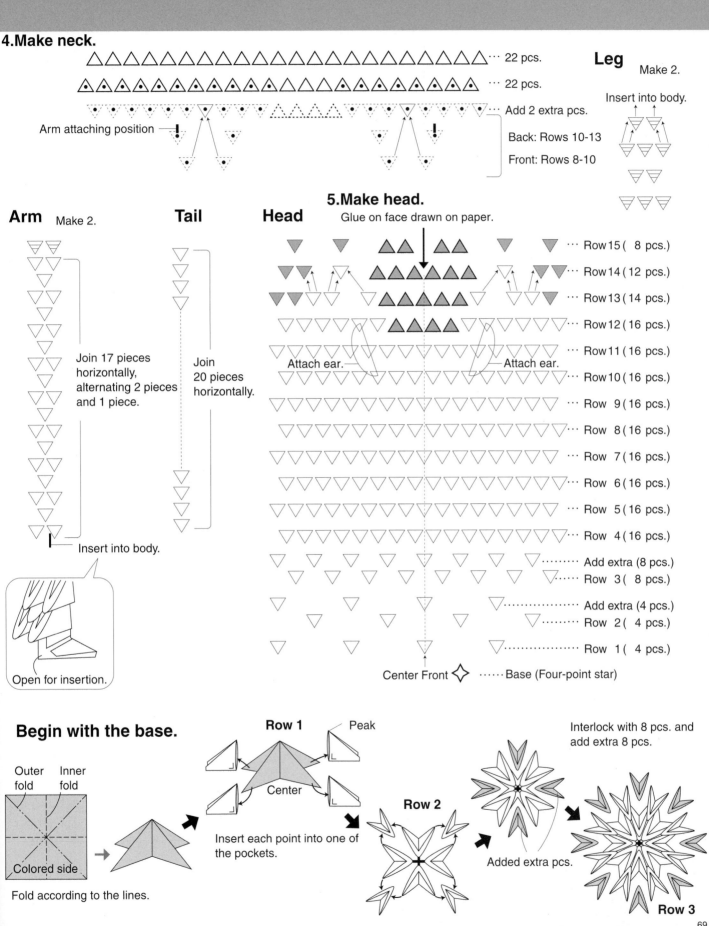

4.Make neck.

△△△△△△△△△△△△△△△△△△△△△△ ··· 22 pcs.

△̇ ··· 22 pcs.

··· Add 2 extra pcs.

Arm attaching position

Back: Rows 10-13

Front: Rows 8-10

Leg   Make 2.

Insert into body.

Arm   Make 2.

Tail

Join 17 pieces horizontally, alternating 2 pieces and 1 piece.

Join 20 pieces horizontally.

Insert into body.

Open for insertion.

Head

5.Make head.

Glue on face drawn on paper.

··· Row 15 (8 pcs.)

··· Row 14 (12 pcs.)

··· Row 13 (14 pcs.)

··· Row 12 (16 pcs.)

··· Row 11 (16 pcs.)

Attach ear.   Attach ear.

··· Row 10 (16 pcs.)

··· Row 9 (16 pcs.)

··· Row 8 (16 pcs.)

··· Row 7 (16 pcs.)

··· Row 6 (16 pcs.)

··· Row 5 (16 pcs.)

··· Row 4 (16 pcs.)

········· Add extra (8 pcs.)

······ Row 3 (8 pcs.)

·········· Add extra (4 pcs.)

········ Row 2 (4 pcs.)

················ Row 1 (4 pcs.)

Center Front ◇ ······ Base (Four-point star)

Begin with the base.

Row 1   Peak

Outer fold   Inner fold

Center

Colored side

Fold according to the lines.

Insert each point into one of the pockets.

Row 2

Interlock with 8 pcs. and add extra 8 pcs.

Added extra pcs.

Row 3

16. Mother Sheep shown on page 18

Materials

364 2"x 3½" rectangles* (white)
  8 2"x 3½" rectangles* (light brown)
  2 2"x 3½" rectangles (white) for ears/bottom
Head: 1 2"W Styrofoam egg
        6" square jersey fabric
Eyes: 2 ¼" plastic joggle eyes

Mouth : felt (grey)
Horns : 2 10"L thick pipe cleaners (silver)
Bang : 1 10"L fine pipe cleaner (white)
Collar : 1 2 ¼" fine pipe cleaner (red)
Tail   : 1 ½" pompon (wihte)
1 miniature bell
Fold rectangles* into triangles.

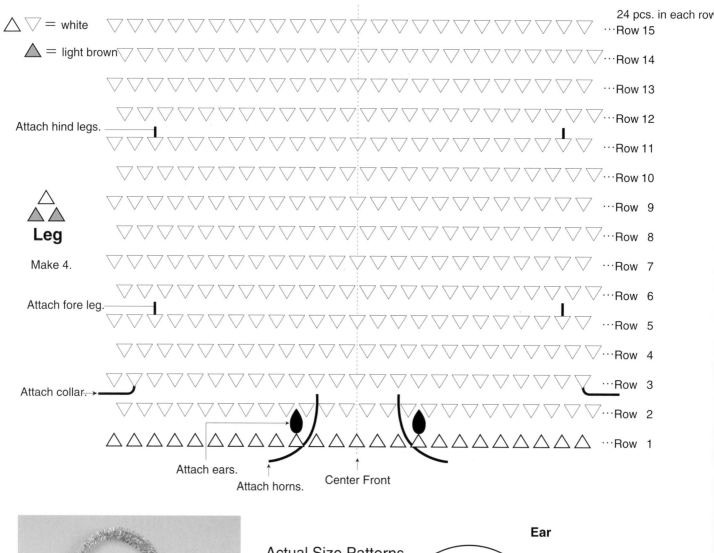

△ ▽ = white

▲ = light brown

△
▲ ▲
Leg

Make 4.

Attach hind legs.

Attach fore leg.

Attach collar.→

Attach ears.

Attach horns.

Center Front

24 pcs. in each row
···Row 15
···Row 14
···Row 13
···Row 12
···Row 11
···Row 10
···Row 9
···Row 8
···Row 7
···Row 6
···Row 5
···Row 4
···Row 3
···Row 2
···Row 1

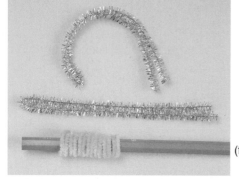

Coil white pipe cleaner using a pencil to make bang. Fold thick pipe cleaner in half, and curl.

Actual Size Patterns

Muzzle

(for both Mother and Child)

Ear

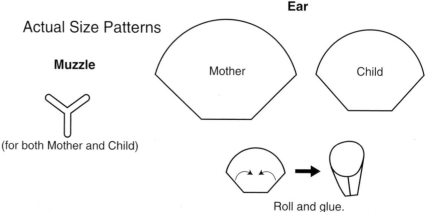

Mother

Child

Roll and glue.

16. Child Sheep shown on page 18

Materials

304 1½" x 2¾" rectangles* (white)

8 1½" x 2¾" rectangles* (light brown)

2 1½" x 2¾" rectangles (white)

Head: 1 2"W Styrofoam egg

4" square jersey fabric

Eyes   : 2 ¼" plastic joggle eyes

Mouth : felt (grey)

Horns : 2 10"L pipe cleaners (silver)

Bang : 1 8"L fine pipe cleaner (white)

Tail   : 1 ½" pompon (wihte)

Fold rectangles* into triangles.

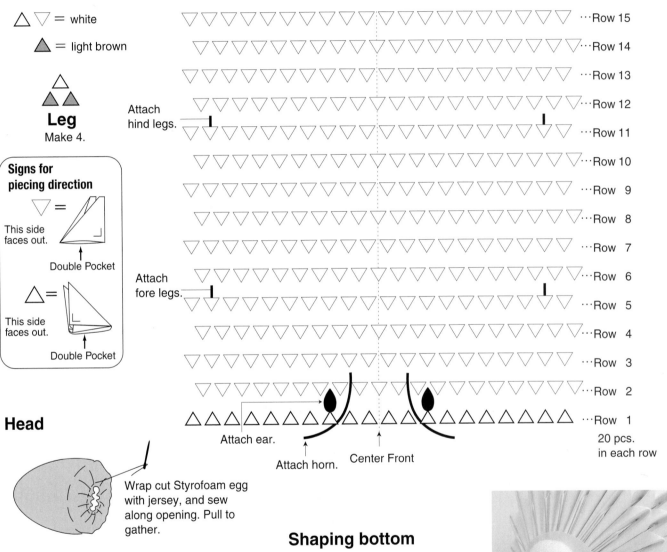

△ ▽ = white

▲ = light brown

Leg
Make 4.

Signs for piecing direction

▽ =

This side faces out.

↑ Double Pocket

△ =

This side faces out.

↑ Double Pocket

Attach hind legs. — ···Row 15 ··· Row 14 ··· Row 13 ··· Row 12 ··· Row 11

··· Row 10 ··· Row 9 ··· Row 8 ··· Row 7 ··· Row 6

Attach fore legs. — ··· Row 5 ··· Row 4 ··· Row 3 ··· Row 2 ··· Row 1

Attach ear.

Attach horn. Center Front

20 pcs. in each row

Head

Wrap cut Styrofoam egg with jersey, and sew along opening. Pull to gather.

Cutting Styrofoam egg

Child approx 1¾" diam.

Mother approx. 2" diam.

Child approx.1⅛"

Mother approx. 1¾"

Shaping bottom

Child: 1½" diam.
Mother: 22" diam.

Glue.   Slit.

Adjust the curve to bottom.

Cover the hole and glue on pompon.

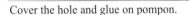

red felt

Cut 2.
Upper crest
Actual Size Pattern

Actual Size Pattern

Lower crest for rooster

Lower crest for hen

Make pleats.

Attach lower tail.

▽▽▽▽▽ ··· Row 17 (5 pcs.)
▽▽▽▽ ··· Row 16 (4 pcs.)
▽▽▽▽▽ ··· Row 15 (5 pcs.)
▽▽▽▽ ··· Row 14 (4 pcs.)
▽▽▽▽▽ ··· Row 13 (5 pcs.)
▽▽▽▽▽▽ ··· Row 12 (6 pcs.)

Attach legs.
▽▽ | ▽ | ▽▽ ··· Row 11 (5 pcs.)
▽▽▽▽▽▽ ···· Row 10 (6 pcs.)

Attach upper tail.
▽▽▽▽▽ ▽▽▽▽▽ ··· Row 9 (12 pcs.)
▽▽▽▽▽▽▽ ▽▽▽▽▽ ··· Row 8 (15 pcs.)

Body ▽▽▽▽▽▽▽▽▽▽▽ ▽ ··· Row 7 (15 pcs.)
▽▽▽▽▽▽▽▽▽▽▽▽▽ ··· Row 6 (15 pcs.)
▽▽▽▽▽△▽▽▽▽▽▽▽ ··· Row 5 (15 pcs.)
▽ ▽ ·······Add extra (2 pcs.)
▽▽▽△△▽ ▽▽▽▽▽▽ ··· Row 4 (13 pcs.)
△ △ ·······Add extra (2 pcs.)
▽ ▽△▽ ▽▽▽▽▽ ··· Row 3 (11 pcs.)
▽ ▽ ·······Add extra (2 pcs.)
▽ ✂ ▽▽▽▽ ··· Row 2 (9 pcs.)
Free flaps
▽ ▽ ▽ ·······Add extra (4 pcs.)
▽ ▽ ▽ ··· Row 1 (4 pcs.)
Center of belly   Center of back
◇ ····· Base (Four-point star)
1¹⁄₂" square

Materials

136 1¹⁄₂" x 2³⁄₄" rectangles* (white)
78 1¹⁄₂" x 2³⁄₄" rectangles* (black)
15 1¹⁄₂" x 2³⁄₄" rectangles* (pattern)
2 1¹⁄₂" x 2³⁄₄" rectangles* (yellow)
1 2" x 3¹⁄₂" rectangle* (red)
4 ³⁄₄" x 1¹⁄₄" rectangles* (yellow)
1 ³⁄₄" x 1¹⁄₄" rectangle (orange)
1 1¹⁄₂" square (white) as base
Felt (red) for crest
2 ¹⁄₄" plastic joggle eyes
Fold rectangles* into triangles.

How to add tail base

Row 9
Row 8
Insert into inner fold.
Row 10
Cover the bottom of Row 9.
Row 11
Free piece
Insert into body.

11 pcs.
▽

7 pcs. 7 pcs.
▽▽ ▽▽
▽▽ ▽▽
▽▽ ▽▽
▽▽ ▽▽
▽▽ ▽▽
▽▽ ▽▽
▽▽▽▽ ··· Row 13 (4 pcs.)
▽▽▽▽▽ ··· Row 12 (5 pcs.)
▽▽▽▽ ··· Row 11 (4 pcs.)
▤▤▤▤▤ ··· Row 10 (5 pcs./Tail base)
▽▽▽▽▽▽▽ ··· Row 9 (Back)

Upper tail (rear view)

Signs for piecing direction

▽ = This side faces out.   Double Pocket

△ = This side faces out.   Double Pocket

Lower tail

Row 18
Row 19
Top view
▽▽▽▽ ··· Row 19 (4 pcs.)
△△△△ ··· Row 18 (4 pcs.)

Wing

Assemble patterned pieces as you work both sides of upper tail.

▽▽▽ ▽▽▽
▽▽▽ ▽▽▽
▽▽▽ ▽▽▽
▽▽▽▽▽▽▽▽ Row 9
▽▽▽▽▽▽▽ Row 8

Row 9 - Row 8 of Body

Body

Belly	Tail	
▼ ▽ ▽	▽ ▼ ▼ ▼ ▽	··· Row 13 (7 pcs.)
▼ ▼ ▼ ▼	▽ ▽ ▽ ▽	··· Row 12 (9 pcs.)
▽ ▽ ▽ ▽ ▽	▽ ▽ ▽ ▽ ▽ ▽	···Row 11 (11 pcs.)
▽ ▽ ▽ ▽ ▽ ▽	▽ ▽ ▽ ▽ ▽	··· Row 10 (11 pcs.)
▽ ▽ ▽ ▽ ▽ ▽	▽ ▽ ▽ ▽ ▽	··· Row 9 (11 pcs.)
▽ ▽ ▽ ▽ ▽ ▽	▽ ▽ ▽ ▽ ▽	··· Row 8 (11 pcs.)
▽ ▽ ▽ △ ▽ ▽	▽ ▽ ▽ ▼ ▽ ▼	··· Row 7 (15 pcs.)
▽ ▽	································	··· Add extra (2 pcs.)
▽ ▽ △△ ▽ ▽	▽ ▽ ▽ ▽ ▽	··· Row 6 (13 pcs.)
▽ ▽ △ ▽ ▽	▽ ▽ ▽ ▽ ▽	··· Row 5 (13 pcs.)
▽ ▽	·················	··· Add extra (2 pcs.)
▽ ▽ ▽ ▽	▽ ▽ ▽ ▽ ▽	··· Row 4 (11 pcs.)
▽ ▽ ▽	▽ ▽ ▽ ▽ ▽	··· Row 3 (11 pcs.)
▽ ▽	················	··· Add extra (2 pcs.)
▽ ▽ ▽	▽ ▽ ▽ ▽	··· Row 2 (9 pcs.)
▽	▽	··· Add extra (4 pcs.)
▽ ▽	▽ ▽	········· Row 1 (4 pcs.)

Attach legs.

Free flaps

Center of belly — Center of back

◇ ··· Base (Four-point star)

1¹⁄₂" square

Wing

▽ ▽	▽ ▽	··· Row 11 (4 pcs.)
▼ ▼ ▽	▽ ▼ ▼	··· Row 10 (6 pcs.)
▼ ▽ ▽	▽ ▽ ▼	··· Row 9 (6 pcs.)
▼ ▼	▼ ▼	··· Row 8 (4 pcs.)

Insert peaks on both sides of belly.

Belly part:
- Row 9 (6 pcs.)
- Row 8 (6 pcs.)
- Row 7 (4 pcs.)

▽ =white
▲ ▼ =black
▽ =black/white pattern

red felt

Upper crest

Actual Size Pattern

Cut 2.

When belly and tail parts are assembled, work wing between them.

Materials   Fold rectangles* into triangles.

- 133 1¹⁄₂" x 2³⁄₄" rectangles* (white)
- 19 1¹⁄₂" x 2³⁄₄" rectangles* (black)
- 14 1¹⁄₂" x 2³⁄₄" rectangles* (pattern)
- 2 1¹⁄₂" x 2³⁄₄" rectangles* (yellow)
- 1 2"x 3¹⁄₂" rectangle* (red)
- 4 ³⁄₄" x 1¹⁄₄" rectangles* (yellow)
- 1 ³⁄₄" x 1¹⁄₄" rectangle (orange)
- 1 1¹⁄₂" square (white) as base

Felt (red) for crest

2 ¹⁄₄" plastic joggle eyes

Common parts for chickens

Leg   Make 2 with yellow pcs.

Insert into body.

1¹⁄₂" x 2³⁄₄"

³⁄₄" x 1¹⁄₄"

Head   Use red felt.

Insert crests and glue.

Tuck pleats between flaps.

Beak

Roll up.

³⁄₄"

Begin with the base.

Outer fold   Inner fold

Colored side

Fold according to the lines.

Row 1   Peak

Center

Insert each point into one of the pockets.

Added extra pcs.

Row 2

Added extra pcs.

Row 3

Interlock with 11 pcs.

Materials

395 1⅛" x 2⅛" rectangles* (white)
8 1½" x 2¾" rectangles* (white)
10 1⅛" squares (white) as base for backbone
8 1¾" x 2⅛" rectangles* (black) for nose and mouth
2 1⅛" squares (black) as base for nose

Neck : ¼" x 4" cardboard
Eyes : Felt (black)
Mouth : Felt (red)
7" ½"W ribbon (pink)
Fold rectangles* into triangles.

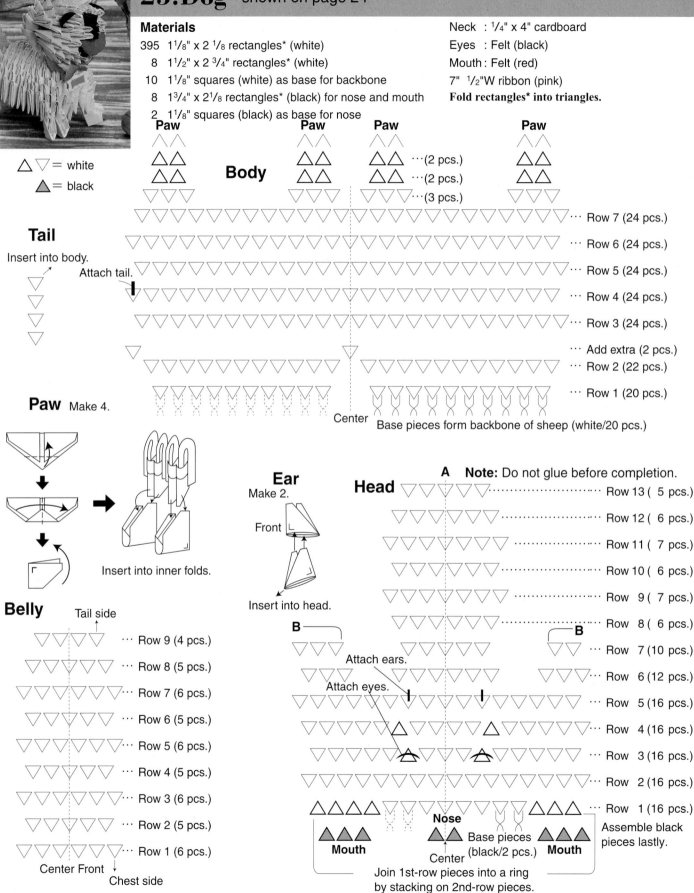

△ ▽ = white
▲ = black

Tail
Insert into body.
Attach tail.

Paw Make 4.
Insert into inner folds.

Belly
Tail side
▽▽▽▽ ··· Row 9 (4 pcs.)
▽▽▽▽▽ ··· Row 8 (5 pcs.)
▽▽▽▽▽▽ ···Row 7 (6 pcs.)
▽▽▽▽▽ ··· Row 6 (5 pcs.)
▽▽▽▽▽▽ ··· Row 5 (6 pcs.)
▽▽▽▽▽ ··· Row 4 (5 pcs.)
▽▽▽▽▽▽ ··· Row 3 (6 pcs.)
▽▽▽▽▽ ··· Row 2 (5 pcs.)
▽▽▽▽▽▽ ··· Row 1 (6 pcs.)
Center Front ↓
Chest side

Body

Paw △ / △△ ···(2 pcs.) / △△ ···(2 pcs.) / ▽▽▽ ···(3 pcs.)

Row 7 (24 pcs.)
Row 6 (24 pcs.)
Row 5 (24 pcs.)
Row 4 (24 pcs.)
Row 3 (24 pcs.)
Add extra (2 pcs.)
Row 2 (22 pcs.)
Row 1 (20 pcs.)

Center
Base pieces form backbone of sheep (white/20 pcs.)

Ear
Make 2.
Front
Insert into head.

Head A **Note:** Do not glue before completion.
▽▽▽ ··· Row 13 (5 pcs.)
··· Row 12 (6 pcs.)
··· Row 11 (7 pcs.)
··· Row 10 (6 pcs.)
··· Row 9 (7 pcs.)
··· Row 8 (6 pcs.)
B ···· Row 7 (10 pcs.)
··· Row 6 (12 pcs.)
Attach ears. ··· Row 5 (16 pcs.)
Attach eyes. ··· Row 4 (16 pcs.)
··· Row 3 (16 pcs.)
··· Row 2 (16 pcs.)
··· Row 1 (16 pcs.)

Nose
Mouth / Base pieces (black/2 pcs.) / **Mouth**
Center
Assemble black pieces lastly.

Join 1st-row pieces into a ring
by stacking on 2nd-row pieces.

Muzzle

Nose : 2 pcs.
Mouth : 6 pcs.

★:black piece

This side faces out.

Front

Signs for piecing direction

$\bigtriangledown$ = This side faces out.

$\bigtriangleup$ = This side faces out.

Double Pocket   Double Pocket

Insert base into Row-1 pieces.

Base

Pull bottom of $\bigtriangledown$ (2 each) and insert to assembling 2 base pieces (black).

Final assembly

Join **A** and **B**.
Secure with glue.

$1\frac{1}{8}$" in diam.

$\frac{1}{4}$"

Make a ring with cardboard.

Glue onto body.

Glue on head.

Tie ribbon around neck.

Body

Actual Size Patterns

Eye

Tongue

Cut felt into shape.

Row 1

Base

Insert peaks of base into pockets of 1st row pieces.

Row 1   **Row 1**

Covered base

Making base

Outer fold   Inner fold

$1\frac{1}{8}$" square

Colored side

Fold according to lines into a four-point star.

Form backbone on Rows 1- 2.

Top view

Insert.

Row 2

Row 1

Row 2

Stand 1st row pieces in a row.

Row 2

Row 2

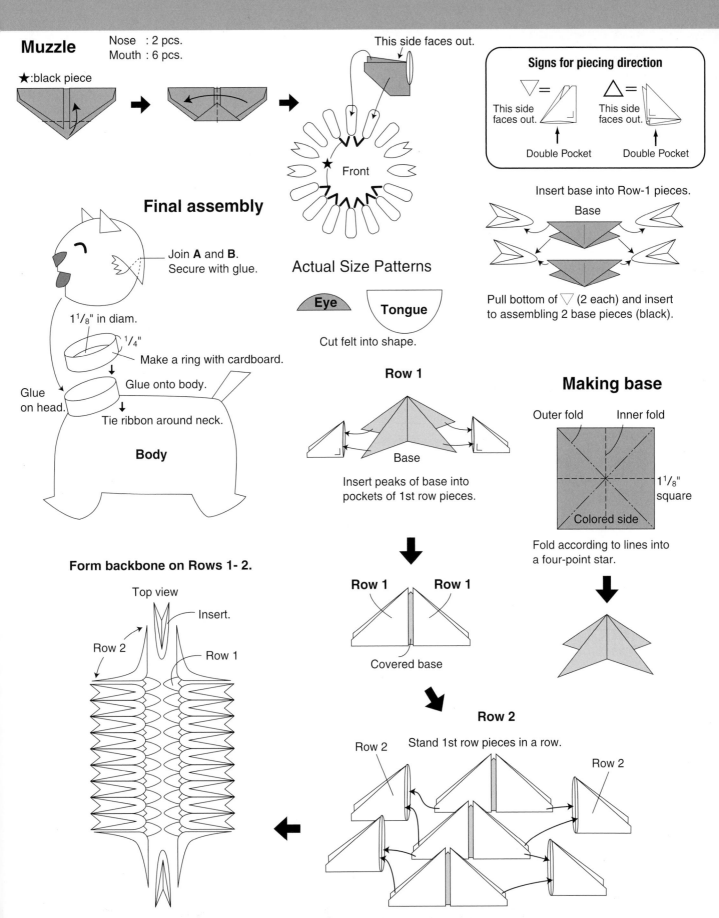

75

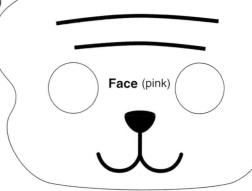

21. Monkey (Three Monkeys) shown on page 21

Materials
1530 1½" x 2¾" rectangles* (light brown)
Felt (light brown for hands/feet, pink for face)
3 silk flower leaves
Permanent marker (brown)
4 ½" plastic joggle eyes
Fold rectangles*
into triangles.

Actual Size Patterns

Ear Cut 4.
(light brown)
Glue onto head.

Hand/Feet
Cut 12.
(light brown)

Face (pink)

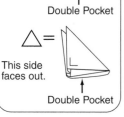

**Signs for
piecing direction**

▽ =
This side
faces out.
Double Pocket

△ =
This side
faces out.
Double Pocket

Head

▽ △ = light brown

Leg

Left   Right

Open bottom piece and
insert inner flaps into body.

Arm

Left   Right

Insert
into
body.

···Row 20
···Row 19
···Row 18
···Row 17
···Row 16
Attach ears. ···Row 15
···Row 14
···Row 13
···Row 12
···Row 11
27 pcs.
in each row

Neck — △△△△△△△△△△△△△△△△△△△△···Row 10

Body

···Row 9
Attach arms. ···Row 8
···Row 7
···Row 6
···Row 5
Attach legs. ···Row 4
···Row 3
···Row 2
···Row 1
20 pcs. in each row

Center Front
Join 20 pieces in a ring.

Increasing on Row 11   Center Front

Row 11 (20 pcs.+ 7 pcs.)

Neck→ Row 10 (20 pcs.)

+ 1 pc. + 1 pc. + 1 pc. + 1 pc. + 1 pc. + 1 pc. + 1 pc.

32.Penguin shown on page 29

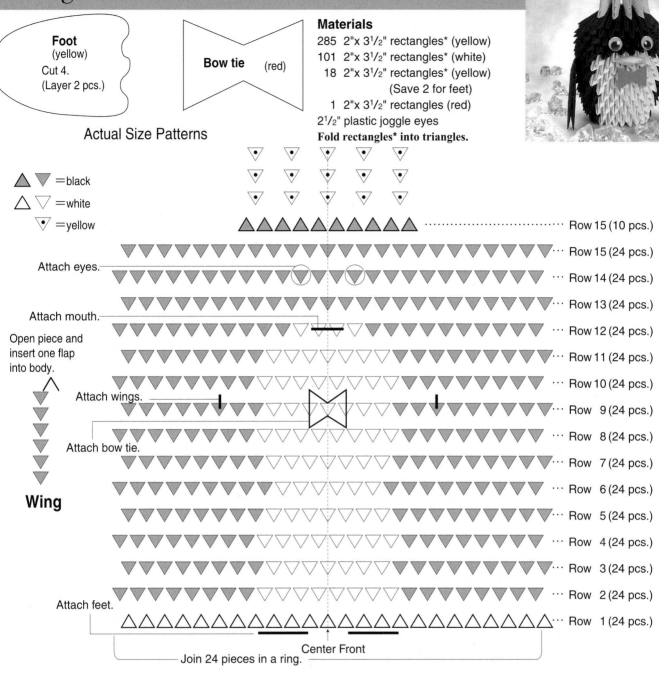

Foot
(yellow)
Cut 4.
(Layer 2 pcs.)

Bow tie (red)

Actual Size Patterns

Materials
285 2"x 3¹/₂" rectangles* (yellow)
101 2"x 3¹/₂" rectangles* (white)
18 2"x 3¹/₂" rectangles* (yellow)
(Save 2 for feet)
1 2"x 3¹/₂" rectangles (red)
2¹/₂" plastic joggle eyes
Fold rectangles* into triangles.

△ ▽ =black
△ ▽ =white
▽ =yellow

Attach eyes.

Attach mouth.

Open piece and
insert one flap
into body.

Attach wings.

Attach bow tie.

Wing

Row 15 (10 pcs.)
Row 15 (24 pcs.)
Row 14 (24 pcs.)
Row 13 (24 pcs.)
Row 12 (24 pcs.)
Row 11 (24 pcs.)
Row 10 (24 pcs.)
Row 9 (24 pcs.)
Row 8 (24 pcs.)
Row 7 (24 pcs.)
Row 6 (24 pcs.)
Row 5 (24 pcs.)
Row 4 (24 pcs.)
Row 3 (24 pcs.)
Row 2 (24 pcs.)
Row 1 (24 pcs.)

Attach feet.

Center Front

Join 24 pieces in a ring.

Mouth

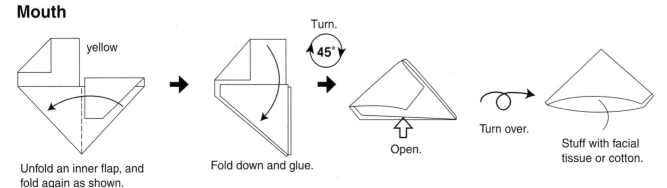

yellow

Unfold an inner flap, and
fold again as shown.

Fold down and glue.

Turn.
45°

Open.

Turn over.

Stuff with facial
tissue or cotton.

Materials

302 1½" x 2¾" rectangles* (white)
106 1½" x 2¾" rectangles* (yellow)
(Save one for bow)
42 1½" x 2¾" rectangles* (orange)
188 1½" x 2¾" rectangles* (flame orange)
2 1½" x 2¾" rectangles (gold) for coin

8 pcs. 4¾" x 4" shiny gold paper for fan
4" square craft paper (black, white, yellow)
Pencil, Permanent marker (black)
Fold rectangles* into triangles.

1.Make pedestal.

Back ··· Row 8 (23 pcs.)
··· Row 7 (24 pcs.)
··· Row 6 (23 pcs.)
··· Row 5 (24 pcs.)
··· Row 4 (23 pcs.)
··· Row 3 (24 pcs.)
··· Row 2 (23 pcs.)
Front ··· Row 1 (24 pcs.)

Fan attaching position

△ ▽ = white
◢ = flame orange
◬ = orange
⌂ = yellow

2.Make fan.

❶ Layer 2 sheets of gold paper colored sides facing out.

❷ Fold lengthwise in half. Repeat twice to make 8 creases.

❸ Unfold and fold into accordion pleats. Glue side sections only.

❹ Make 4 in the same manner.

❺ Join by gluing side sections together.
Glue

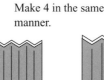

Actual Size Patterns

Right whiskers (black)

Left whiskers(black)

Eyes(black)

Nose(yellow)

Right Ear (white)

Left Ear (white)

Bow
Cut from yellow rectangle.
1½" x 2¾"
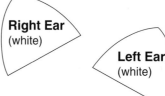

Laminate 2 gold pieces and cut out oval.

Ancient gold coin

3. Make head.

Attach ears. Glue on bows. Attach ears.

22 pcs. in each row

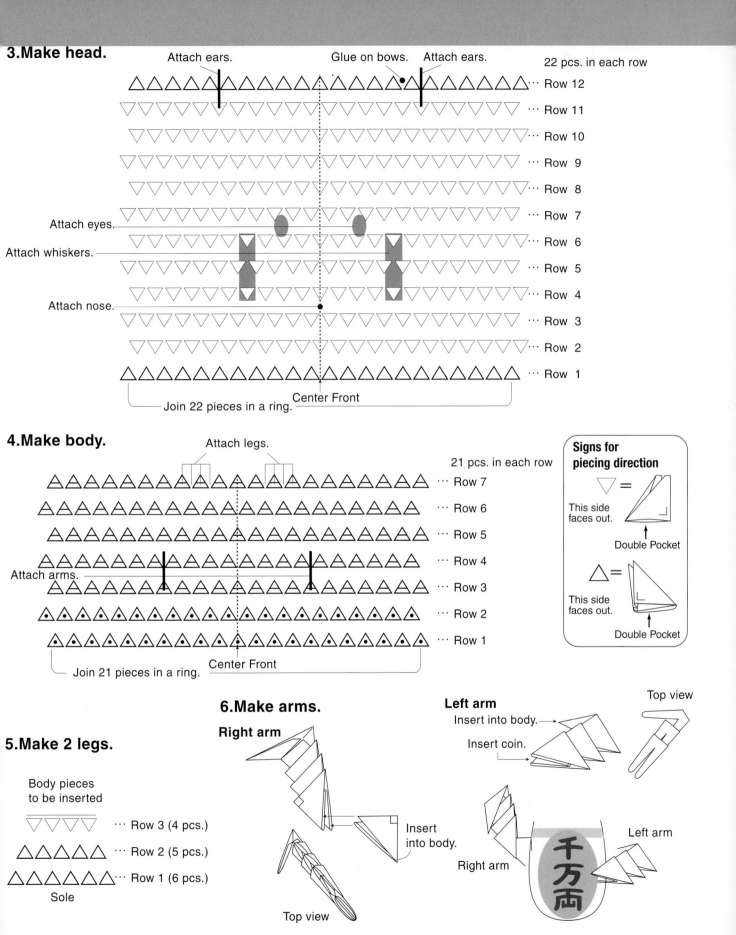

Row 12
Row 11
Row 10
Row 9
Row 8
Row 7
Attach eyes.
Row 6
Attach whiskers.
Row 5
Row 4
Attach nose.
Row 3
Row 2
Row 1

Center Front

Join 22 pieces in a ring.

4. Make body.

Attach legs.

21 pcs. in each row

Row 7
Row 6
Row 5
Row 4
Attach arms.
Row 3
Row 2
Row 1

Center Front

Join 21 pieces in a ring.

Signs for piecing direction

▽ =

This side faces out.

↑ Double Pocket

△ =

This side faces out.

↑ Double Pocket

5. Make 2 legs.

Body pieces to be inserted

▽▽▽▽ ··· Row 3 (4 pcs.)

△△△△△ ··· Row 2 (5 pcs.)

△△△△△△ ··· Row 1 (6 pcs.)

Sole

6. Make arms.

Right arm

Insert into body.

Top view

Left arm

Insert into body. →

Insert coin. →

Top view

Right arm

Left arm

千万両

79

36. Santa Claus shown on page 32

Materials

189 2"x 3 1/2" rectangles* (white)

22 2"x 3 1/2" rectangles* (skin)

(Save one for hands)

360 2"x 3 1/2" rectangles* (red)

36 2"x 3 1/2" rectangles* (black)

Belt: 16"x 3/8" craft paper (black)

Felt (white for beard, cuffs and button, red for hat, black for eyes, yellow for nose)

1 1/2" pompon (white)

Fold rectangles* into triangles.

△ ▽ =white

▲ ▼ =red

▽ =skin color

△• ▼• =black

Hand/Arm

Actual Size Patterns on opposite page

2 red pcs.   white felt cuff

Arm Make 2.

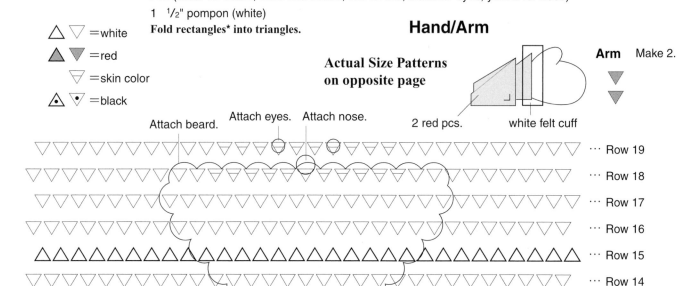

Attach beard.   Attach eyes.   Attach nose.

··· Row 19
··· Row 18
··· Row 17
··· Row 16
··· Row 15
··· Row 14
··· Row 13
··· Row 12

Attach arms.

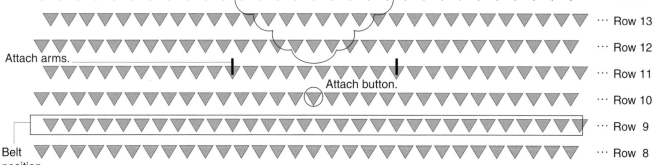

Attach button.

··· Row 11
··· Row 10
··· Row 9

Belt position. (3/8"W)

··· Row 8
··· Row 7
··· Row 6

··· Row 5
··· Row 4

··· Row 3
··· Row 2
··· Row 1

30 pcs. in each row

Join 30 pieces in a ring.

34. Tulip shown on page 30

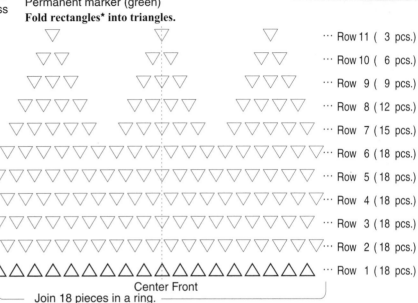

Tulip assembly

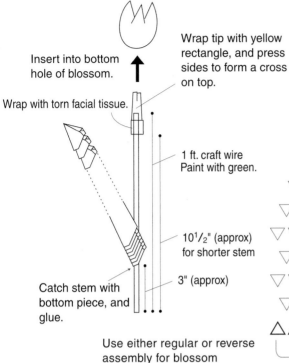

Insert into bottom hole of blossom.

Wrap tip with yellow rectangle, and press sides to form a cross on top.

Wrap with torn facial tissue.

1 ft. craft wire
Paint with green.

$10^1/_2$" (approx)
for shorter stem

3" (approx)

Catch stem with bottom piece, and glue.

Use either regular or reverse assembly for blossom

Materials for 3 Tulips

153	$1^1/_2$" x $2^3/_4$" rectangles*	(yellow)
153	$1^1/_2$" x $2^3/_4$" rectangles*	(red)
153	$1^1/_2$" x $2^3/_4$" rectangles*	(pink)
60	2"x $3^1/_2$" rectangles*	(green)
3	$1^1/_2$" x $2^3/_4$" rectangles	(yellow)

3 $1/_4$"W x 1 ft.L craft wires
Permanent marker (green)

Fold rectangles* into triangles.

Row 11 (3 pcs.)
Row 10 (6 pcs.)
Row 9 (9 pcs.)
Row 8 (12 pcs.)
Row 7 (15 pcs.)
Row 6 (18 pcs.)
Row 5 (18 pcs.)
Row 4 (18 pcs.)
Row 3 (18 pcs.)
Row 2 (18 pcs.)
Row 1 (18 pcs.)

Center Front
Join 18 pieces in a ring.

Santa Claus Patterns

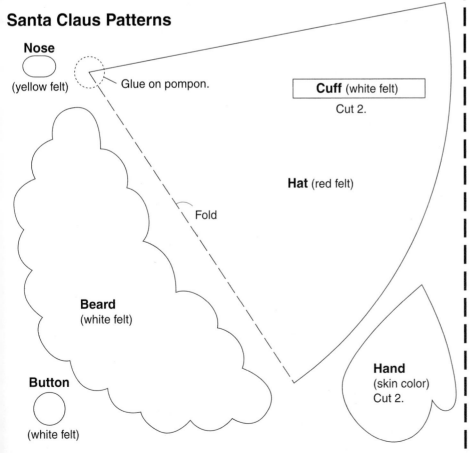

Nose
(yellow felt)

Glue on pompon.

Cuff (white felt)
Cut 2.

Hat (red felt)

Fold

Beard
(white felt)

Button

(white felt)

Hand
(skin color)
Cut 2.

Leaf

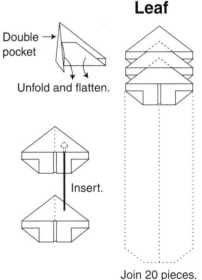

Double pocket

Unfold and flatten.

Insert.

Join 20 pieces.

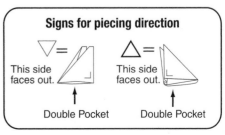

Signs for piecing direction

▽ = This side faces out.

△ = This side faces out.

Double Pocket

Double Pocket

37. Snowman shown on page 32

Materials

410 2"x 3 1/2" rectangles* (white)

Felt (black for features, orange for nose, blue and
   yellow for mittens, red for bucket)

1 1/8" x 12" jersey fabric for scarf

Fold rectangles* into triangles.

Bucket (red)
Bottom part

**Signs for
piecing direction**

$\bigtriangledown$ =

This side
faces out.

Double Pocket

$\bigtriangleup$ =

This side
faces out.

Double Pocket

Actual Size Patterns

Bucket (red)

Side part

Glue.

*Glue onto white piece and insert into body.

Mitten

Cut 1 each in
blue and yellow.

$\bigtriangleup$ $\bigtriangledown$ =white

Attach eyebrows.

··· Row 17

··· Row 16

Attach eyes.

··· Row 15

··· Row 14

··· Row 13

Attach mouth.

··· Row 12

··· Row 11

Head

Neck ··· Row 10

Attach mittens(*). ··· Row 9

··· Row 8

··· Row 7

··· Row 6

Body ··· Row 5

··· Row 4

··· Row 3

··· Row 2

··· Row 1

Center Front

24 pcs.
in each row

Join 24 pieces in a ring.

Actual Size Patterns

Eye
(black)

Cut 2.

Nose
(orange)

Mouth (black)

Eyebrow
(black)

Cut 2.

26 Wild Boar shown on page 25

Materials per Large Boar

349 2"x 3½" rectangles* (dark brown)

43 2"x 3½" rectangles* (light brown)

1 2"x 3½" rectangle (light brown)

2 ⅜" plastic joggle eyes

Fold rectangles* into triangles.

Materials per Baby Boar

349 1½" x 2¾" rectangles* (yellow)

43 1½" x 2¾" rectangles* (dark brown)

1 1½" x 2¾" rectangle (muzzle/fangs)

2 ¼" plastic joggle eyes

Fold rectangles* into triangles.

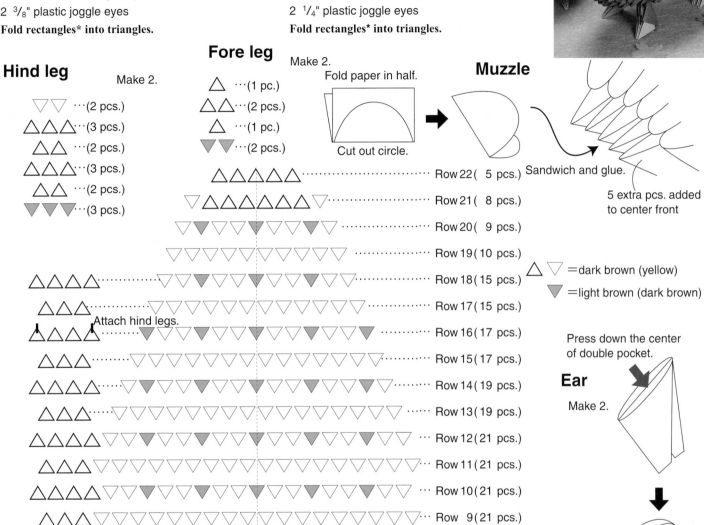

Hind leg
Make 2.

Fore leg
Make 2.
Fold paper in half.

Cut out circle.

Muzzle

Sandwich and glue.

5 extra pcs. added to center front

$\triangle$ $\triangledown$ = dark brown (yellow)

$\blacktriangledown$ = light brown (dark brown)

Press down the center of double pocket.

Ear
Make 2.

Row 22 (5 pcs.)
Row 21 (8 pcs.)
Row 20 (9 pcs.)
Row 19 (10 pcs.)
Row 18 (15 pcs.)
Row 17 (15 pcs.)
Row 16 (17 pcs.)
Row 15 (17 pcs.)
Row 14 (19 pcs.)
Row 13 (19 pcs.)
Row 12 (21 pcs.)
Row 11 (21 pcs.)
Row 10 (21 pcs.)
Row 9 (21 pcs.)
Add extra (5 pcs.)
Row 8 (16 pcs.)
Row 7 (16 pcs.)
Row 6 (16 pcs.)
Row 5 (16 pcs.)
Row 4 (16 pcs.)
Add extra (4 pcs.)
Row 3 (12 pcs.)
Row 2 (12 pcs.)
Row 1 (12 pcs.)
Assemble lastly (5 pcs.).

Attach hind legs.

Attach fore legs.

Attach ears.

Attach eyes.

Center Front

Attach fangs.

Join 1st-row pieces into a ring by stacking on 2nd-row pieces.

Fang
Make 2.

½"

Fold to form sharp point.

Using specially processed papers

Although we have recommended ordinary papers such as origami paper, recycled flyer and copy papers to make 3D Origami projects, some specially processed papers such as "Pearl-color Origami Paper" can expand the possibility of this craft. They can create a shiny, smoother and rounded surface rather than the regular "spiky" and neat surface. These papers with pearlized, roughly textured surface and soft, pliable touch are thicker than regular origami paper but they are on the contrary hard to crease. For this reason, when folding such paper into triangle, fold without any ease which is a must to regular papers. Prepare ample triangular pieces and leave them stacked together to keep the shape until use.

If using a regular paper for projects designed for this type of paper, remember that the finished size becomes slightly

How to fold pearl-color origami

Work in the same manner until Step 7 on page 2.

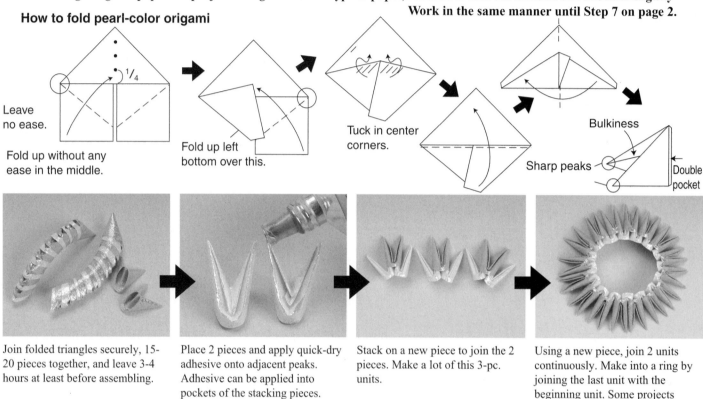

Leave no ease.

Fold up without any ease in the middle.

Fold up left bottom over this.

Tuck in center corners.

Bulkiness

Sharp peaks

Double pocket

Join folded triangles securely, 15-20 pieces together, and leave 3-4 hours at least before assembling.

Place 2 pieces and apply quick-dry adhesive onto adjacent peaks. Adhesive can be applied into pockets of the stacking pieces.

Stack on a new piece to join the 2 pieces. Make a lot of this 3-pc. units.

Using a new piece, join 2 units continuously. Make into a ring by joining the last unit with the beginning unit. Some projects require reversed direction on the 1st row.

Final assembly of Pony

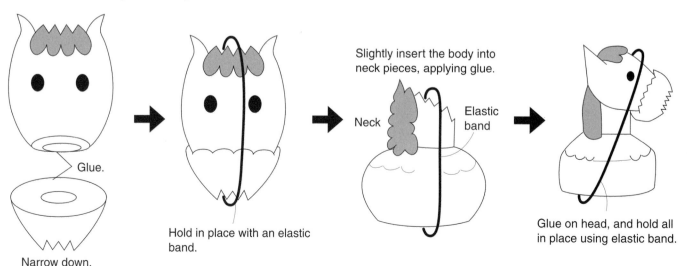

Glue.

Narrow down.

Hold in place with an elastic band.

Slightly insert the body into neck pieces, applying glue.

Neck

Elastic band

Glue on head, and hold all in place using elastic band.

15. Horse (Pony) shown on page 18

Neck

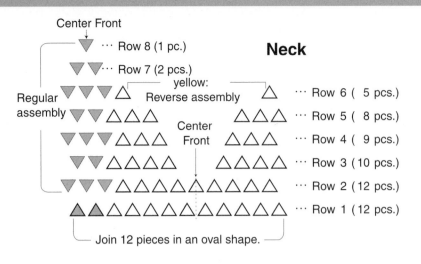

Center Front
··· Row 8 (1 pc.)
··· Row 7 (2 pcs.)
yellow:
Reverse assembly ··· Row 6 (5 pcs.)
Regular assembly
··· Row 5 (8 pcs.)
Center Front ··· Row 4 (9 pcs.)
··· Row 3 (10 pcs.)
··· Row 2 (12 pcs.)
··· Row 1 (12 pcs.)
Join 12 pieces in an oval shape.

△▽ = yellow
▲▽ = blue

Materials
366 1" x 2¼" rectangles* (yellow) pearly origami
36 1" x 2¼" rectangles* (blue) pearly origami
2 ¼" button (black) for eyes
Fold rectangles* into triangles.

Tail

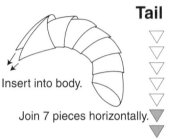

Insert into body.

Join 7 pieces horizontally.

▽
▽
▽
▽
▽
▽
▼
▼

Body

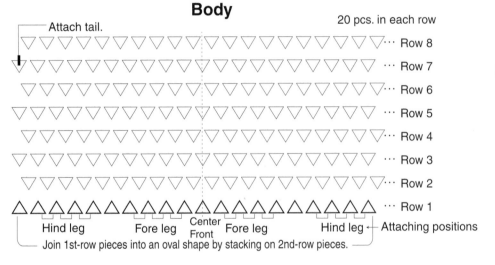

Attach tail.
··· Row 8
··· Row 7
··· Row 6
··· Row 5
··· Row 4
··· Row 3
··· Row 2
··· Row 1

20 pcs. in each row

Hind leg | Fore leg | Center Front | Fore leg | Hind leg ← Attaching positions

Join 1st-row pieces into an oval shape by stacking on 2nd-row pieces.

Leg   Make 4.

▽▽▽ ··· Row 3 (3 pcs.)
▽▽ ··· Row 2 (2 pcs.)
▼▼▼ ··· Row 1 (3 pcs.)

Insert into underneath of body.

Head

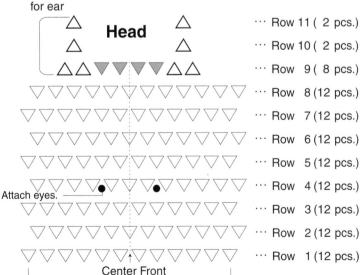

Reversed assembly for ear
··· Row 11 (2 pcs.)
··· Row 10 (2 pcs.)
··· Row 9 (8 pcs.)
··· Row 8 (12 pcs.)
··· Row 7 (12 pcs.)
··· Row 6 (12 pcs.)
··· Row 5 (12 pcs.)
Attach eyes. ··· Row 4 (12 pcs.)
··· Row 3 (12 pcs.)
··· Row 2 (12 pcs.)
··· Row 1 (12 pcs.)
Center Front
Join 1st-row pieces into a ring by stacking on 2nd-row pieces.

Muzzle

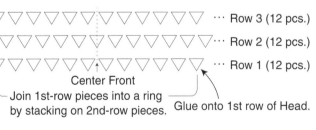

··· Row 3 (12 pcs.)
··· Row 2 (12 pcs.)
··· Row 1 (12 pcs.)

Center Front
Join 1st-row pieces into a ring by stacking on 2nd-row pieces.
Glue onto 1st row of Head.

Signs for piecing direction

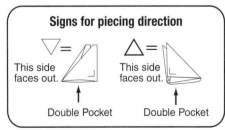

▽ = This side faces out.   △ = This side faces out.

Double Pocket   Double Pocket

18. Sheep (Lamb) shown on page 19

Materials

391 1" x 2¼" rectangles* (white) pearly origami
 20 1" x 2¼" rectangles* (yellow) pearly origam
 2   ¼" buttons (black) for eyes
 1   ⅜" pompon (white) for tail

See page 84 and fold rectangles* into triangles.

Center Back

Body Tail attaching position

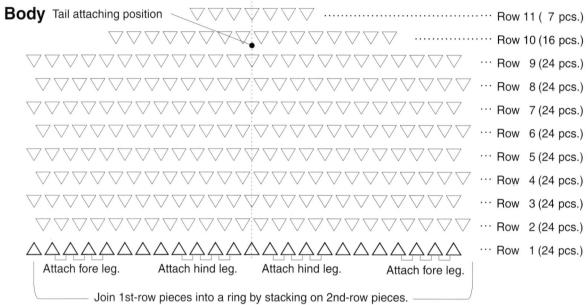

··· Row 11 (7 pcs.)
··· Row 10 (16 pcs.)
··· Row 9 (24 pcs.)
··· Row 8 (24 pcs.)
··· Row 7 (24 pcs.)
··· Row 6 (24 pcs.)
··· Row 5 (24 pcs.)
··· Row 4 (24 pcs.)
··· Row 3 (24 pcs.)
··· Row 2 (24 pcs.)
··· Row 1 (24 pcs.)

Attach fore leg.   Attach hind leg.   Attach hind leg.   Attach fore leg.

Join 1st-row pieces into a ring by stacking on 2nd-row pieces.

Head

··· Row 8
··· Row 7
··· Row 6
··· Row 5
··· Row 4
··· Row 3
··· Row 2
··· Row 1

Attach eye.   Center Front   Attach eye.

Join 1st-row pieces into a ring
by stacking on 2nd-row pieces.

Mouth

△△△△△△△△△△ ··· Row 2 (10 pcs.)
△△△△△△△△△△ ··· Row 1 (10 pcs.)

Center

Join 1st-row pieces into a ring
by stacking on 2nd-row pieces
reversing piece direction.

Horn

Make 2.

Row 2 (10 pcs.)
Row 1 (10 pcs.)

14 pcs. in each row

Join 10 pieces
horizontally.

Apply glue as you join each
piece, shape and let dry.

Leg Make 4.

··· Insert into underneath of body.
··· Row 2 (3 pcs.)
··· Row 1 (2 pcs.)

△ ▽ =white
�▼ =yellow

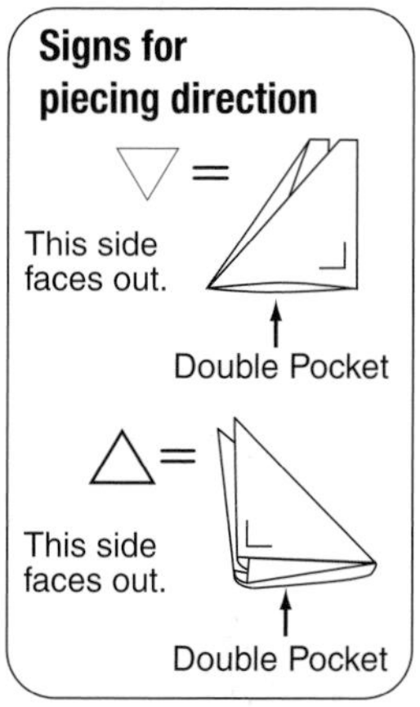

Mouth

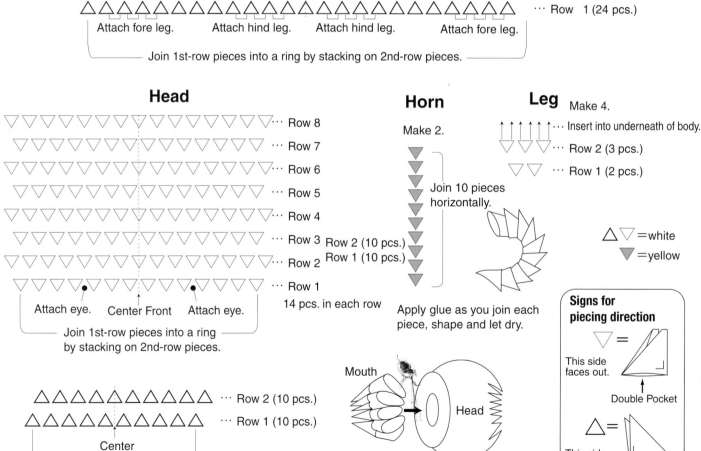

Head

Glue 1st row of mouth onto 1st
row of head.

Signs for piecing direction

▽ =
This side faces out.
Double Pocket

△ =
This side faces out.
Double Pocket

20. Girl Monkey shown on page 21

Head

Attach ear.   Attach ear.

··· Row 11 (18 pcs.)
··· Row 10 (18 pcs.)
··· Row 9 (18 pcs.)
··· Row 8 (18 pcs.)
··· Row 7 (18 pcs.)
··· Row 6 (18 pcs.)
··· Row 5 (18 pcs.)
··· Row 4 (18 pcs.)
··· Row 3 (18 pcs.+ 1 pc.)
··· Row 2 (18 pcs.)
··· Row 1 (18 pcs.)

▽ = pink
▽ (white outline) = white
▼ = yellow

Thrust a yellow piece. Center Front

Join 1st-row pieces into a ring
by stacking on 2nd-row pieces.

Materials

366   1" x 2¼" rectangles* (pink)
      pearly origami (Save 4 for ears)
30   1" x 2¼" rectangles* (white)
      pearly origami
1   1" x 2¼" rectangle* (yellow)
      pearly origami
2   ⅓" button (black) for eyes
Cardboard
See page 84 and fold rectangles* into triangles.

Body

Attach arm.   Attach arm.   14 pcs. in each row

···Row 8
···Row 7
···Row 6
···Row 5
···Row 4
···Row 3
···Row 2
···Row 1

Insert legs.   Center Front

Join 1st-row pieces into a ring by stacking on 2nd-row pieces.

Attach tail.

Tail / Arm

Make 3.

Join 20 pieces
horizontally.

Apply glue as you
join pieces, and curl
as shown. Insert a
wooden toothpick
into the 1st piece,
and secure with glue.
Insert this end into
body.

Leg   Make 2.

Insert into body.

▼ ▼ ··· Row 4 (2 pcs.)
▼ ··· Row 3 (1 pc.)
▼ ▼ ··· Row 2 (2 pcs.)
▼ ··· Row 1 (1 pc.)

Actual Size Patterns

Ear Cut 2.

Ear Cut 2.

Ear Make 2.

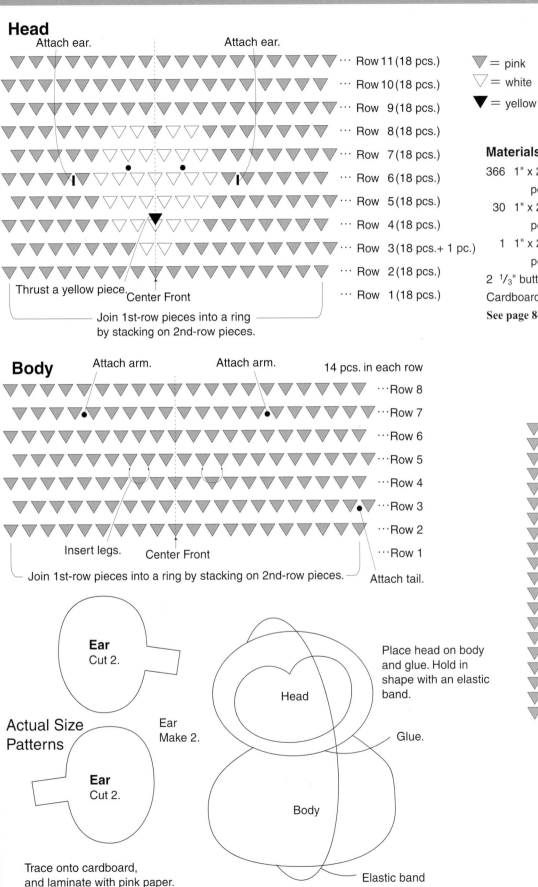

Head

Body

Place head on body
and glue. Hold in
shape with an elastic
band.

Glue.

Elastic band

Trace onto cardboard,
and laminate with pink paper.

87

24.Rooster (Parent) shown on page 23

Materials

353 1" x 2¹/₄" rectangles* (white) pearly origami
  3 1" x 2¹/₄" rectangles* (yellow) pearly origami
  2 1" x 2¹/₄" rectangles* (red) pearly origami for crest
  2 ¹/₄" plastic joggle eyes
See page 84 and fold rectangles* into triangles.

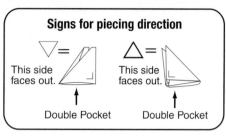

Signs for piecing direction

▽ = This side faces out.   △ = This side faces out.
Double Pocket   Double Pocket

For wing costruction, use reverse assembly.

Wing

Attach neck. △▽ = white ▽ = yellow

Attach tail.

Wing

Attach tail.

Ⓐ Ⓐ Ⓑ Ⓒ   Ⓒ Ⓑ

Row13 (2 pcs.)
Row12 (5 pcs.)
Row11 (8 pcs.)
Row10 (11 pcs.)
Row 9 (14 pcs.)
Row 8 (24 pcs.)
Row 7 (24 pcs.)
Row 6 (24 pcs.)
Row 5 (24 pcs.)
Row 4 (24 pcs.)
Row 3 (24 pcs.)
Row 2 (24 pcs.)
Row 1 (24 pcs.)

Attach leg of 1 yellow pc. Center Front Attach leg of 1 yellow pc.

Join 1st-row pieces into a ring by stacking on 2nd-row pieces.

Attaching neck

Neck

Chest

Neck

Attach eyes. △ ··· Row 15 (1 pc.)
●△I△● ··· Row 14 (2 pcs.)
Attach crest △ ··· Row 13 (1 pc.)
to head and chin. △△ ··· Row 12 (2 pcs.)
△ ··· Row 11 (1 pc.)
△△ ··· Row 10 (2 pcs.)
△ ··· Row 9 (1 pc.)
△△ ··· Row 8 (2 pcs.)
△ ··· Row 7 (1 pc.)
△△ ··· Row 6 (2 pcs.)
△ ··· Row 5 (1 pc.)
△△ ··· Row 4 (2 pcs.)
△ ··· Row 3 (1 pc.)
△△ ··· Row 2 (2 pcs.)
△ ··· Row 1 (1 pc.)

Tail Make 2 each.

Ⓐ
△ Join 20 pieces horizontally.
△ Make 2.

Ⓑ
△ Join 16 pieces horizontally.
△ Make 2. Ⓒ
△ Join 14 pieces horizontally.
△ Make 2.

Attaching foot

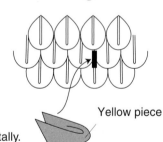

Yellow piece

Attaching crest

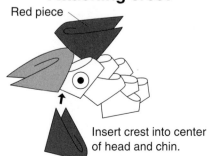

Red piece

Insert crest into center of head and chin.

24. Rooster (Child) shown on page 23

Materials
93 1" x 2¼" rectangles* (white) pearly origami
3 1" x 2¼" rectangles* (yellow) pearly origami
2 1" x 2¼" rectangles* (red) pearly origami for crest
2 ¼" plastic joggle eyes
See page 84 and fold rectangles* into triangles.

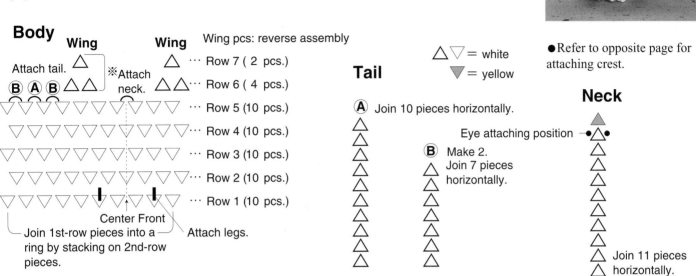

Body

Wing   **Wing**

Attach tail.

Wing pcs: reverse assembly

··· Row 7 (2 pcs.)
··· Row 6 (4 pcs.)
··· Row 5 (10 pcs.)
··· Row 4 (10 pcs.)
··· Row 3 (10 pcs.)
··· Row 2 (10 pcs.)
··· Row 1 (10 pcs.)

※Attach neck.

Ⓑ Ⓐ Ⓑ

Center Front
Attach legs.

Join 1st-row pieces into a ring by stacking on 2nd-row pieces.

Tail

Ⓐ Join 10 pieces horizontally.

Ⓑ Make 2.
Join 7 pieces horizontally.

△▽ = white
▼ = yellow

● Refer to opposite page for attaching crest.

Neck

Eye attaching position →●△●

Join 11 pieces horizontally.

Holstein: Materials and Color Chart   ●Instructions on pages 64-65.

Head

Materials
421 1½" x 2¾" rectangles* (white)
164 1½" x 2¾" rectangles* (black)
10 ¾" x 1½" rectangles* (black) for tail
12 ¾" x 1½" rectangles* (pink) for horns

1 ¾" miniature cowbell
2 ⅜" plastic joggle eyes
See page 84 and fold rectangles* into triangles.

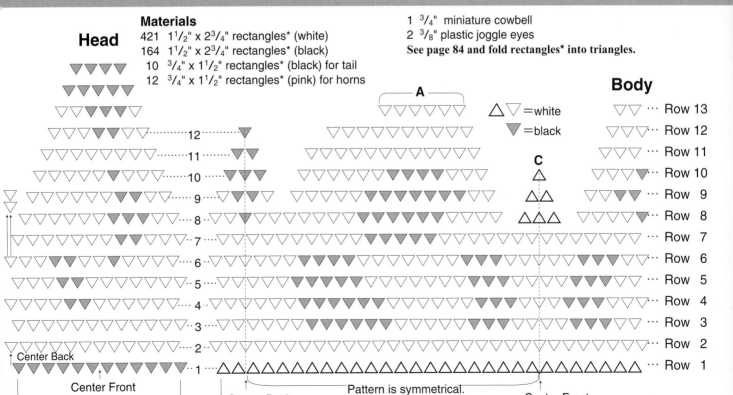

△▽ =white
▼ =black

Body

···	Row 13
···	Row 12
···	Row 11
···	Row 10
···	Row 9
···	Row 8
···	Row 7
···	Row 6
···	Row 5
···	Row 4
···	Row 3
···	Row 2
···	Row 1

A

C

12
11
10
9
8
7
6
5
4
3
2
1

Center Back
Center Front

Join 1st-row pieces into a ring by stacking on 2nd-row pieces.

Pattern is symmetrical.
Center Back   Center Front
Join 1st-row pieces into a ring by stacking on 2nd-row pieces.

27. Dragon Boat shown on page 26

Materials

296 1" x 2¼" rectangles* (blue) pearly origami

174 1" x 2¼" rectangles* (yellow) pearly origami

56 1" x 2¼" rectangles* (pink) pearly origami

3" x 7" (approx.) cardboard

2 ¼" plastic joggle eyes

9 2mm round beads (gold)

1 ⅜"H metallic cap (gold)

10 3"L strands fine cording

2 metallic ornaments (gold)

2 miniature pagodas (gold and silver), optional

See page 84 and fold rectangles* into triangles.

Row 14 (6 pcs.)
Row 13 (8 pcs.)
Row 12 (10 pcs.)
Row 11 (12 pcs.)
Row 10 (14 pcs.)
Row 9 (16 pcs.)
Row 8 (26 pcs.)
Row 7 (36 pcs.)
Row 6 (46 pcs.)
Row 5 (56 pcs.)
Row 4 (56 pcs.)
Row 3 (56 pcs.)
Row 2 (56 pcs.)
Row 1 (56 pcs.)

Continued to lower chart

Center Back

Join 1st-row pieces into a ring by stacking on 2nd-row pieces.

△ ▽ =blue

▼ =yellow

▽• =pink

Cut an oval shape from cardboard, and adjust the shape of boat by using it as a guide. Glue the bottom of boat onto the cardboard.

Row 14 (6 pcs.)
Row 13 (8 pcs.)
Row 12 (10 pcs.)
Row 11 (12 pcs.)
Row 10 (14 pcs.)
Row 9 (16 pcs.)
Row 8 (26 pcs.)
Row 7 (36 pcs.)
Row 6 (46 pcs.)
Row 5 (56 pcs.)
Row 4 (56 pcs.)
Row 3 (56 pcs.)
Row 2 (56 pcs.)
Row 1 (56 pcs.)

Center Front

Join 1st-row pieces into a ring by stacking on 2nd-row pieces.

Neck

Make 2.

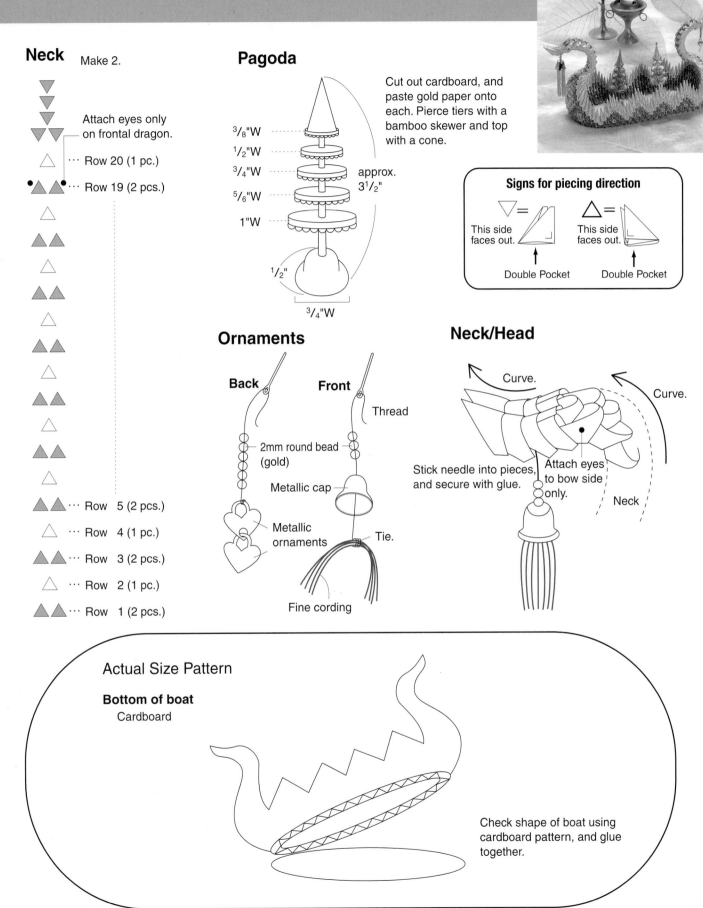

Attach eyes only on frontal dragon.

··· Row 20 (1 pc.)

··· Row 19 (2 pcs.)

··· Row 5 (2 pcs.)

··· Row 4 (1 pc.)

··· Row 3 (2 pcs.)

··· Row 2 (1 pc.)

··· Row 1 (2 pcs.)

Pagoda

Cut out cardboard, and paste gold paper onto each. Pierce tiers with a bamboo skewer and top with a cone.

$3/8$"W

$1/2$"W

$3/4$"W

$5/6$"W

1"W

approx. 3$1/2$"

$1/2$"

$3/4$"W

Signs for piecing direction

▽ = This side faces out.   △ = This side faces out.

Double Pocket   Double Pocket

Ornaments

Back   **Front**

Thread

2mm round bead (gold)

Metallic cap

Metallic ornaments

Tie.

Fine cording

Neck/Head

Curve.   Curve.

Stick needle into pieces, and secure with glue.

Attach eyes to bow side only.

Neck

Actual Size Pattern

Bottom of boat
Cardboard

Check shape of boat using cardboard pattern, and glue together.

28.Crane Basket shown on page 27

Materials

558 1" x 2 ¼" rectangles* (white) pearly origami

2 1" x 2¼" rectangles* (red) pearly origami

2 ¼" plastic joggle eyes

4 ¼" square cardboard

See page 84 and fold rectangles* into triangles.

Shaping

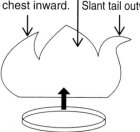

Stand wings upright.

Slant chest inward. | Slant tail outwa

Apply glue as you piece, check the shape, and let dry.

Cut out a circle from cardboard, and glue.

Tail

Left wing

Chest

Right wing

Row 15 (6 pcs.)

Row 14 (10 pcs.)

△···Row 13 (14 pcs.)

△ ···Row 12 (18 pc

△△ △···Row 11 (22 pc

△△ △···Row 10 (26 pc

Same as Right wing

△△△ △···Row 9 (30 pc

△△△ △···Row 8 (34 pc

···Row 7 (38 pc

···Row 6 (38 pc

···Row 5 (38 pc

···Row 4 (38 pc

···Row 3 (38 pc

···Row 2 (38 pc

···Row 1 (38 pcs

Center Front

Join 1st-row pieces into a ring by stacking on 2nd-row pieces.

Neck

Reverse assembly (seen from front) Insert all 4 peaks into 1 piece.

△ ▽ = white

△ = red

··· Row 25 (1 pc. red)

···Row 24 (2 pcs.)

Eye •△ △• Eye

Repeat "1 pc., 2 pcs." until 24th row is done.

··· Row 4 (2 pcs.)

··· Row 3 (1 pc.)

··· Row 2 (2 pcs.)

··· Row 1 (1 pc.)

Beak

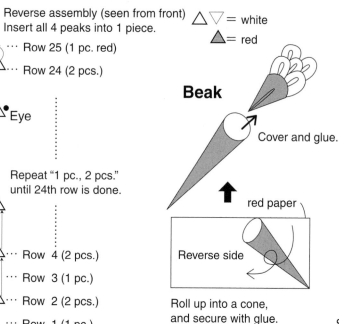

Cover and glue.

red paper

Reverse side

Roll up into a cone, and secure with glue.

Handle Regular assembly

Insert into left wing and secure with glue.

··· Row 64 (2 pcs.)

··· Row 63 (1 pc.)

Repeat "1 pc., 2 pcs." until 64 rows are joined.

··· Row 4 (2 pcs.)

··· Row 3 (1 pc.)

··· Row 2 (2 pcs.)

··· Row 1 (1 pc.)

Stack onto right wing and secure with glue.

Handle pcs.

Left wing pcs.

Handle pcs.

Right wing pcs

29.Basket shown on page 27

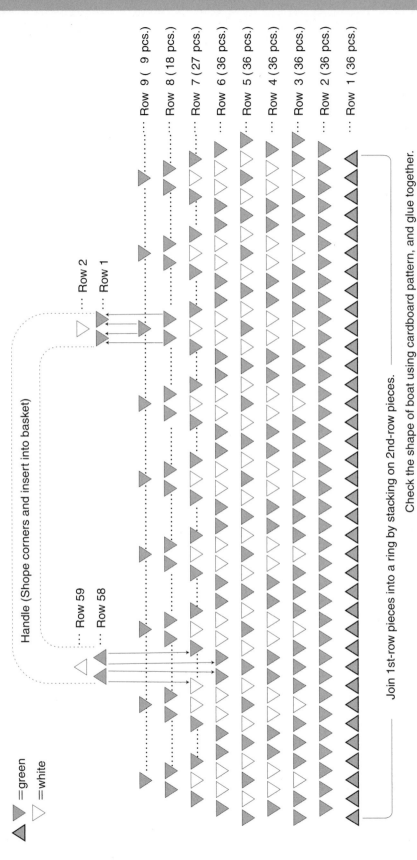

Row 9 (9 pcs.)
Row 8 (18 pcs.)
Row 7 (27 pcs.)
Row 6 (36 pcs.)
Row 5 (36 pcs.)
Row 4 (36 pcs.)
Row 3 (36 pcs.)
Row 2 (36 pcs.)
Row 1 (36 pcs.)

··· Row 2
··· Row 1

Handle (Shope corners and insert into basket)

··· Row 59
··· Row 58

Join 1st-row pieces into a ring by stacking on 2nd-row pieces.

Check the shape of boat using cardboard pattern, and glue together.

▶ =green
▷ =white

Materials

258 1" x 2¼" rectangles* (green)
     pearly origami
101 1" x 2¼" rectangles* (white)
     pearly origami
4" square (approx.) cardboard
See page 84 and fold rectangles* into triangles.

Handle

▽▽ ··· Row 59 (2 pcs.)
▽ ··· Row 58 (1 pc.)
▽▽ ··· Row 57 (2 pcs.)
▽ ··· Row 56 (1 pc.)
▽▽ ··· Row 55 (2 pcs.)

Join 59 rows horizontally.

▽ ··· Row 6 (1 pc.)
▽▽ ··· Row 5 (2 pcs.)
▽ ··· Row 4 (1 pc.)
▽▽ ··· Row 3 (2 pcs.)
▽ ··· Row 2 (1 pc.)
▽▽ ··· Row 1 (2 pcs.)

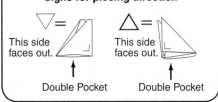

Signs for piecing direction

▽ =   △ =
This side faces out.   This side faces out.
↑   ↑
Double Pocket   Double Pocket

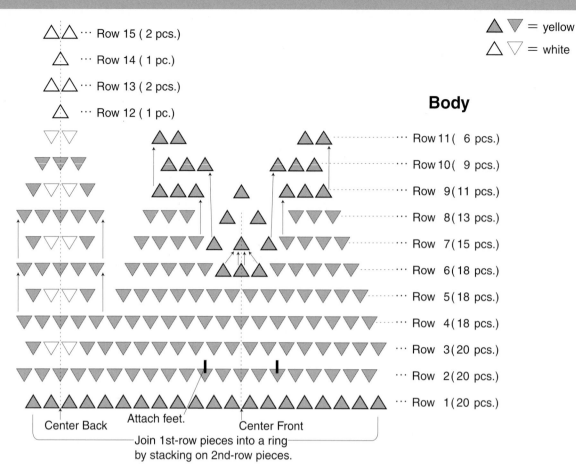

Row 15 (2 pcs.)
Row 14 (1 pc.)
Row 13 (2 pcs.)
Row 12 (1 pc.)

△ ▽ = yellow
△ ▽ = white

Body

Row 11 (6 pcs.)
Row 10 (9 pcs.)
Row 9 (11 pcs.)
Row 8 (13 pcs.)
Row 7 (15 pcs.)
Row 6 (18 pcs.)
Row 5 (18 pcs.)
Row 4 (18 pcs.)
Row 3 (20 pcs.)
Row 2 (20 pcs.)
Row 1 (20 pcs.)

Center Back
Attach feet.
Center Front
Join 1st-row pieces into a ring
by stacking on 2nd-row pieces.

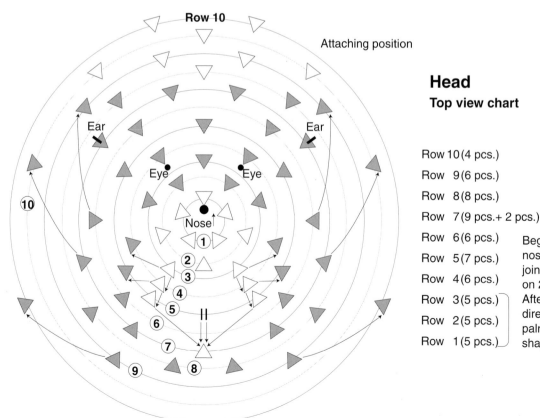

Row 10
Attaching position

Ear
Ear
Eye
Eye
Nose
⑩
①
②
③
④
⑤
⑥
⑦
⑧
⑨

Head
Top view chart

Row 10 (4 pcs.)
Row 9 (6 pcs.)
Row 8 (8 pcs.)
Row 7 (9 pcs.+ 2 pcs.)
Row 6 (6 pcs.)
Row 5 (7 pcs.)
Row 4 (6 pcs.)
Row 3 (5 pcs.)
Row 2 (5 pcs.)
Row 1 (5 pcs.)

Begin with 5 center pcs, e.g. nose attaching position, and join into a ring by stacking on 2nd-row pieces. After assembling in regular direction, hold tightly in your palm to form a pine cone shape.

Materials

333   1" x 2¼" rectangles* (yellow) pearly origami
 77   1" x 2¼" rectangles* (white) pearly origami
  2   ¼" buttons (black) for eyes
  1   ⅙" button (black) for nose
  4   ¾" Mizuhiki cord (black) for whiskers
  1   wooden toothpick
See page 84 and fold rectangles* into triangles.

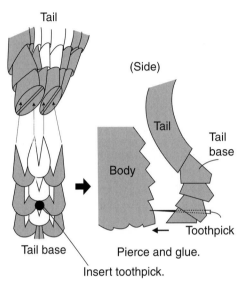

Tail (Front view)

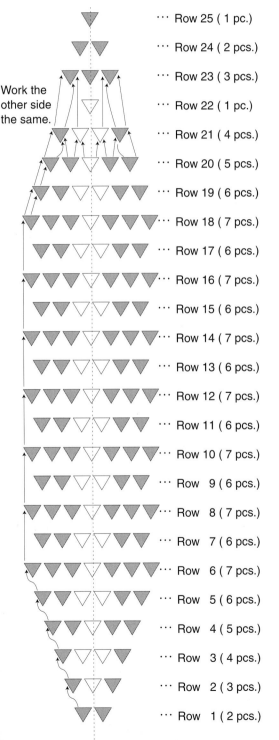

Work the other side the same.

··· Row 25 (1 pc.)
··· Row 24 (2 pcs.)
··· Row 23 (3 pcs.)
··· Row 22 (1 pc.)
··· Row 21 (4 pcs.)
··· Row 20 (5 pcs.)
··· Row 19 (6 pcs.)
··· Row 18 (7 pcs.)
··· Row 17 (6 pcs.)
··· Row 16 (7 pcs.)
··· Row 15 (6 pcs.)
··· Row 14 (7 pcs.)
··· Row 13 (6 pcs.)
··· Row 12 (7 pcs.)
··· Row 11 (6 pcs.)
··· Row 10 (7 pcs.)
··· Row 9 (6 pcs.)
··· Row 8 (7 pcs.)
··· Row 7 (6 pcs.)
··· Row 6 (7 pcs.)
··· Row 5 (6 pcs.)
··· Row 4 (5 pcs.)
··· Row 3 (4 pcs.)
··· Row 2 (3 pcs.)
··· Row 1 (2 pcs.)

Tail base
(seen from backside)

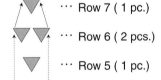

▽ ··· Row 7 (1 pc.)
▼▼ ··· Row 6 (2 pcs.)
▽ ··· Row 5 (1 pc.)
▼▼ ··· Row 4 (2 pcs.)
▽ ··· Row 3 (1 pc.)
▼▼ ··· Row 2 (2 pcs.)
△ ··· Row 1 (1 pc.)

Hand Make 2.

··· Row 7 (1 pc.)
··· Row 6 (2 pcs.)
··· Row 5 (1 pc.)
··· Row 4 (2 pcs.)
··· Row 3 (3 pcs.)
··· Row 2 (2 pcs.)
··· Row 1 (1 pc.)

Insert toothpick.

Tail assembly

Tail

(Side)

Tail

Tail base

Body

Tail base

Insert toothpick.

Pierce and glue.

Toothpick

Foot Make 2.

2 pcs.

Insert between 2nd row pieces of body.

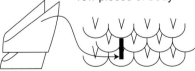

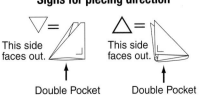

Signs for piecing direction

▽ = 〈This side faces out.〉
Double Pocket

△ = 〈This side faces out.〉
Double Pocket

95

31.Brilliant Peacock shown on page 29

Materials

283 1" x 2¼" rectangles* (green) pearly origami

62 1" x 2¼" rectangles* (yellow) pearly origami

(Save 1 for beak)

16 1" x 2¼" rectangles* (pink)

Silk flower stamens

2 ¼" plastic joggle eyes

See page 84 and fold rectangles* into triangles.

Neck

Reverse assembly (when seen from fron[t]

△ ⋯ Row 16 (1 pc. yellow)

Attach eyes.

Join 15 green pieces horizontally.

Neck pcs.

Chest pcs.

Tail

▽ Row 12 (24 pcs.)

▽ Row 11 (23 pcs.)

▽ Row 10 (24 pcs.)

▽ Row 9 (23 pcs.)

Row 8 (22 pcs.)

Using only one pocket of each piece, increase to 22 pieces.

Row 7 (11 pcs.)

Row 6 (10 pcs.)

Row 5 (9 pcs.)

Row 4 (8 pcs.)

Row 3 (7 pcs.)

Row 2 (6 pcs.)

Row 1 (5 pcs.)

Shaping body

Slant chest inward.

Curl wings outward.

Make joint by assembling 4 pieces horizontally. Make 3 and stack on body pieces.

Insert into body.

Beak

yellow paper

Reverse side

Roll up into a cone, and secure with glue.

Stamens

yellow

Cover and glue.

△ ▽ = green

△ ▼ = yellow

▽ = pink

Signs for piecing direction

▽ = This side faces out. Double Pocket

△ = This side faces out. Double Pocket

Backside of tail feather assembly

Chest

Row 11 (2 pcs.) ⋯ ▽ ▽

Wing
(Reverse assembly)

Wing
(Reverse assembly)

△ ⋯ ▽ ▼ ▽ ⋯ △ ⋯ Row 10 (5 pcs.)

△ △ ⋯ ▽ ▼ ▼ ▽ ⋯ △ △ ⋯ Row 9 (8 pcs.)

△ △ △ ⋯ ▽ ▽ ▼ ▽ ▽ ⋯ △ △ △ ⋯ Row 8 (11 pcs.)

Attach tail.

△ △ △ △ ▽ ▽ ▼ ▽ ▽ △ △ △ △ ⋯ Row 7 (14 pcs.)

Body

▽ ⋯ Row 6 (20 pcs.)

▽ ⋯ Row 5 (20 pcs.)

▽ ⋯ Row 4 (20 pcs.)

▽ ⋯ Row 3 (20 pcs.)

▽ ⋯ Row 2 (20 pcs.)

▽ ⋯ Row 1 (20 pcs.)

↑ Center Front

Join 1st-row pieces into a ring by stacking on 2nd-row pieces.

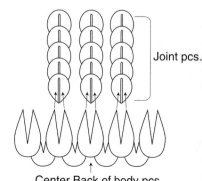

Joint pcs.

Center Back of body pcs.